I0008728

SUDDEN CHANGE

SUDDEN CHANGE

✦

A Play-by-Play Account of My Transformation

Jerry Glover

iUniverse, Inc.

New York Lincoln Shanghai

SUDDEN CHANGE
A Play-by-Play Account of My Transformation

Copyright © 2008 by Jerry Glover

All rights reserved. No part of this book may be used or reproduced by any means, graphic, electronic, or mechanical, including photocopying, recording, taping or by any information storage retrieval system without the written permission of the publisher except in the case of brief quotations embodied in critical articles and reviews.

iUniverse books may be ordered through booksellers or by contacting:

iUniverse
2021 Pine Lake Road, Suite 100
Lincoln, NE 68512
www.iuniverse.com
1-800-Authors (1-800-288-4677)

Because of the dynamic nature of the Internet, any Web addresses or links contained in this book may have changed since publication and may no longer be valid.

The views expressed in this work are solely those of the author and do not necessarily reflect the views of the publisher, and the publisher hereby disclaims any responsibility for them.

ISBN: 978-0-595-46958-1 (pbk)
ISBN: 978-0-595-91242-1 (ebk)

Printed in the United States of America

Contents

Introduction ix

CHAPTER 1   The Turning Point 1

CHAPTER 2   Twenty Years of New Life 3

CHAPTER 3   Outside the Camp 5

CHAPTER 4   Roots in the Soil 7

CHAPTER 5   Programmed to Fail 10

CHAPTER 6   Bubba 13

CHAPTER 7   Change 14

CHAPTER 8   The Blue Devils 19

CHAPTER 9   This Is Alabama Football 21

CHAPTER 10   Other Stories from Inside the Camp 25

CHAPTER 11   More from the Capstone 29

CHAPTER 12   Funerals and Deaths 33

CHAPTER 13   More About "Class Tells" 35

CHAPTER 14   Three Types of People 38

CHAPTER 15   Fatigue Makes Cowards of Us All 42

CHAPTER 16   More About the Real—the Authentic 44

CHAPTER 17   Structure Works Against People 46

CHAPTER 18   The Holy Spirit Rejects Structure 49

CHAPTER 19   Courage 52

CHAPTER 20   Two Outdated Words: Authority and Integrity 54

CHAPTER 21   The Rod of Correction. 58

CHAPTER 22   Poverty, Work, and Eating. 62

CHAPTER 23   Racism and Civil Rights. 65

CHAPTER 24   Proving God 69

CHAPTER 25   I Am Who I Am. 73

CHAPTER 26   Why Are There Still Monkeys?. 75

CHAPTER 27   Persecution. 77

CHAPTER 28   Hardness of Heart 80

CHAPTER 29   A Definition of Grace 82

CHAPTER 30   The Changed Life 84

CHAPTER 31   Religiosity 87

CHAPTER 32   What Balanced Believing Believes 90

CHAPTER 33   The Watered-Down Gospel. 93

CHAPTER 34   Altar Calls, Baptism, and Counts 96

CHAPTER 35   Rocky Balboa—Hope 99

CHAPTER 36   Purpose 102

CHAPTER 37   The Will of God 106

CHAPTER 38   Mother Teresa 110

CHAPTER 39   A Simple Solution 112

CHAPTER 40   Cynic or Prophet 114

CHAPTER 41   Why Did It Take So Long? 117

CHAPTER 42   To Whom Shall We Go? 119

CHAPTER 43   It's with the Heart 121

CHAPTER 44   Conclusion 124
Special Thanks To 131

Introduction

Way back in the days when I was the head student manager under legend-ary Coach Paul "Bear"Bryant at the University of Alabama, we were always given the same list of objectives before going onto the field. Proba-bly the most prolific point was that we were to be alert to sudden change. In the football world, sudden change is the situation where the possession of the ball changes due to a fumble, an interception, or a blocked kick. The sudden change can be a violent, and even dangerous, time. Players who were moving in one direction are abruptly changed in motion and direction. Unusual, and possibly traumatic, things can occur during sud-den change.

I've selected the title, *Sudden Change*, for this book because this expres-sion and its connotations best describe a condition into which my life was thrust twenty years ago. It's not important that people hear about the things that occurred to me per say, but it is important that I bring to light the principles that were involved. In this book I attempt to give an accu-rate play-by-play account of my sudden change from being a very dis-turbed, lost sinner to a transformed man twenty years in the making. To my knowledge, I've never known of anyone attempting a similar account.

Without judging or placing blame on anyone, let me say that in my journey since the sudden change few people have personally helped me in the area of concrete guidance. During a time of frequent stress, there were people who loved me through these tough times, but there just weren't many people out there who could give advice. Could this be the way God intends? Moses, Paul, and even Jesus were probably out in the desert with no shoulder to cry on or anyone to point their way. Once their preparation time was accomplished however they had much to say and much to offer. That's about the position in which I now find myself.

This book is a myriad of writings on varied topics, such as football, my own personal opinions and beliefs, and the current serious condition of our world. You will notice that I also discuss in some detail our tendency today to operate in denial of truth or in a state of delusion. It is my personal knowledge of this denial or delusional state that gives me the insight into it. Of the twenty years of my journey, I spent approximately half of that time denying some still ugly stains. I was fixed safely as a believer in Jesus Christ, but there were some ugly matters lurking beneath the surface of my outward righteousness. It is this state that I wish to discuss for I think there is much of it out there today—people hiding behind a religious mask or even a one-time experience with God and a cleaned-up exterior. This condition is the sole underlying purpose for this book. This condition must be prevalent today. Just look at the current state of the church, even the so called blood bought church. If we were truly open to God and not asleep in delusion, then we'd see mass repentance. To truly see God is to willfully comply with His commands., and the greatest of these commands is that we love our brothers. This is rarely done today. Claiming to know God while still walking without brotherly love is irrefutable evidence of this state of delusion. For my involvement in this state of denial of the true facts, I've confessed and repented. Can I ask others to at least be open to the fact that they may be guilty also. This book will reveal many of the ways in which this delusion operates;I invite you to jump right into it, I promise you that this will be rewarding.

I'm not fooling myself into thinking that I am now an expert on everything. However, I am an expert on the forces and events that I have experienced in my life after my time of sudden change. My life since that time has not been that nice, quiet little life that some expect. The enemies, which are my old soulish self, the world political and religious system, and the actual devil, are out there and they are formidable.

This book will find its place with those people who are open to receive this type of message. CNN's Wolf Blitzer and his sidekick, Jack Cafferty, will be of those who will not receive this message. Wolf, Jack, and I do have one thing in common, however: we all feel that we're going downhill fast in this society. Wolf and Jack think that their answer, that of exposing the weak links, will purify our world. They think that they have the perfect solution: replace the weak with the strong. My solution is much simpler and more affective. My solution is this: just make a sincere commitment to Jesus Christ. Having done this, you'll then enter into the point of sudden change which is the only pause that truly refreshes.

My hope is that this highly unusual book will be both enjoyable and beneficial to you. May God bless you as He has me and my entire household.

1

The Turning Point

About twenty years ago, on June 2, 1987, a sudden change in my life occurred. I was sitting up with my father in his hospital room where we had just been told that same morning that he had liver cancer and would soon die. I decided to take a walk down for coffee and some serious meditation. My life of forty-four years was turned about as upside down as one could be. In fact, I even harbored thoughts that things were so bad that it might be better to end my life.

How can I explain what occurred next in that coffee shop? I can only tell what I know. While contemplating the dilemma of my own condition and now my father's death, a question popped into my mind. How could things for me be so bad while my father, who had received Jesus about eight years earlier, always seemed to overcome and even prosper? Then, the answer came up sort of like a cartoon caption in the air. The answer was that it was this Jesus who he had been following and trying to talk with me about.

Now, here's the puzzling part of this. At this time, I called out to God and said in effect, *If you're real and can do for me what you've done for my dad, then I want to come, too.* Being the big shot that I had tried so hard to become, I actually said that I would be willing to speak up for Him. God would be lucky to have someone like me speak for Him. How great was that?

You see, for forty-four years I had been living a life dedicated to denying and hiding the person whom I really was and attempting to paint a false picture of whom I would like to be. I had made some big splashes, but they were only splashes. In the words of my first boss after college, Coach Wyman Townsel, I was a "look-good loser." Wyman used the term to describe all those good-looking football players on the sidelines, while our team was not performing well on the field.

As I made this commitment to God, a very strange peace fell upon me. It seemed to me that all would be well now, although I knew I must stick to my commitment. I then walked to the elevators and into my father's room. My father had awakened and said, "Jerry, I'd like to talk to you." My reply was, "Dad, I know what you want. It has just happened downstairs." We then had great fellowship as he told me about the Jesus he had received.

The next day, my dad asked his pastor to come up while I was there to ask me what are called the "saving questions." We all assumed that my point of salvation had occurred either the previous night or while answering the questions that day. However, after over twenty years in Christ, I now know that this was only the *beginning of repentance,* the time of deciding that a change was needed and committing to make that change. The point of beginning, the point of repentance, brought with it some mighty supernatural results. The biggest of these results was peace and contentment, but there were other big ones, too. I was miraculously healed forever of severe alcoholism that very first day. I also have never again thought of pulling over in front of a moving truck. My dad, in fact, died seven weeks later, but what a seven-week period it was for me.

In conclusion to this thought, on the day that my father had requested his pastor to come by, his brother and sister-in-law were also in the room. At that time, I made the statement that my father should write a book about his amazing life. His reply was that he didn't think there was enough time. Well, after twenty years of walking with Jesus, sometimes seemingly alone, I'm now writing the book. My hope is that this book will bring glory to God and the memory of my father, Coach Jim Glover, who broke the curse of the enemy over our household by becoming the first believer, but not the last.

2

Twenty Years of New Life

For twenty years now, I have attempted within my limited abilities and strengths to follow the commitment I made in the coffee shop at Holy Name of Jesus Hospital in Gadsden, Alabama. These years have been filled with miracles and wonders from God. From the very beginning, there has been a very real presence of God around me and my family. I am absolutely, unchangeably, wholeheartedly attempting to follow this God. He is so real. How could anyone of a sound mind whom having witnessed the happenings around me not do this? I've very often been foolish in my life, but I'm no fool. Being foolish can be temporary; being a fool is permanent.

It is for these reasons that I am doing the unthinkable—I am writing this book. In this book, I attempt to express in words the real-life situations that to me prove the existence of Jehovah God, His son Jesus Christ, and His Holy Spirit. In these twenty years, I have seen many attempts to prove God's existence through the conjuring up of miracles and such. I've even seen some genuine miracles, which I'm certain were not from our God, but from the enemy. I saw a lady once bouncing in the air through no effort of her own on the stage platform. It is my opinion that today in the United States, there is an absence of the true consecration from men that would allow God's hand to perform the miracles that were done by the early church. Man now takes the credit. My feeling is that we are too far into the worship of self now to allow this from God.

The type proofs which I can offer to prove God's existence are through the changes and the miracles in the lives around me. I sincerely believe that today in America, as at all times in all places, God is seeking the pure heart, one who will be true to His word and His promises. In order to

3

develop such a person, much polishing and correction is required, super-natural events will definitely accompany such a process. This polishing and correction occurs after man's initial approach to God. This process has lasted for twenty years in my life and shows no signs of being completed.

Both God and the enemy operate supernatural powers. God desires a clean vessel, and in order for Him to be able to receive such a vessel, much refinement is required. The miracles from God, which I have witnessed, have been in the order of breakthroughs or gifts. The miracles from the enemy have been in the realm of exposing hidden sins or taking away those things which must be removed. This last type of miracle explains the taking away of my business, which was an idol for me.

This book contains stories and real-life situations, which have occurred during my twenty years as a Christian and the sixty-four years of my life. I am no theologian, but I am an entrepreneurial type who knows the real when he sees it. I've witnessed very much, which I have concluded as not being real and of little value. I have also seen the real, and I'm following Him as best that I am able to do.

3

Outside the Camp

"And so Jesus also suffered outside the city gate to make the people holy through His own blood. Let us then go to Him, outside the camp bearing the disgrace He bore" (Hebrews 13:12–13). The initial title for the book was changed by necessity. As the book was evolving, it was apparent that the first selected title, Outside the Camp, was not the proper one, but only a secondary title of some significance.

The secondary title of this book is drawn from the above passage for two reasons. First, all that I have learned and witnessed in my walk with God through Jesus tells me that we are to bear His cross, suffer His reproach which was outside the camp, die to our old ways (self), and take on His nature. To be totally honest, very little is spoken today of these things. Dying is not a popular topic.

Second, my entire life, both before receiving Jesus and then after His entrance, has been outside the camp. Prior to becoming a Christian, my subconscious mind told me that I was a Bubba (we'll talk more about Bubba later). I attempted with everything in my being not to be a Bubba. I even succeeded somewhat at not being a Bubba, a non mainstream person,when my company, Promar, had grown fairly large. People then would give at least lip service to my being okay. However, I wasn't okay, and I thank God that He saw someone else inside the old me.

Since becoming a Christian I have continued, although not intentionally, to be an outside camper, another person who operates outside the mainstream. I just couldn't keep quiet about the things that had happened to me. I just couldn't settle into that seeming sterile life which I saw and heard around me. Looking back, I guess I was acting as a chip off the old block. My father, after coming to the Lord and shedding a huge burden of guilt, couldn't keep quiet either. He even got up at his induction ceremony at the Alabama Sports Hall of Fame, alongside such greats as Hank Aaron and Paul W. Bryant, and told the people at the induction about the one who lived here on Earth for thirty-two years and carried the sins of the world to the cross. Then, this Jesus, after successfully disarming Satan at the cross, was resurrected and now sits at the right hand of the Father to make intercession for the saints.

4

Roots in the Soil

Let me make this concession: I come from a background of cotton farming and football, not academia. You'll see phrases like the one Yogi Berra is famous for, "It ain't over till it's over," and "When you're up to your chin in elephant dung, don't worry about the rabbit pills," and "If you're scared, say you're scared," and on and on. The people up the line from me, my ancestors,dwelt on the basics and that's how I dwell also. Don't be too concerned about perfection when your life is very far from it now. Take care of first things first.

My ancestors, the ones of whom I know, come from the Tuscaloosa area in Alabama. My father's people were sharecroppers in Hale County; my mother's family managed a small general store in the coal mining area north of Tuscaloosa. From what I have learned, my father's family led a very meager life, in part due to my grandfather's compulsive nature and quick temper. This family must have changed farms at least once a year. My father literally hated farming, and once he saw a football, he never looked back.

On the other extreme, my mother's people were very well-respected, stable members of their little community of Coaling, Alabama, where my grandfather was a charismatic Baptist song leader, as well as a thirty-five-year member of the county school board. I can see him now hitting two hymnals together as he led singing. My grandmother was the greatest, most loving person I have ever known. Everyone called her Aunt Claude.

Some of my earliest memories of life were in Tarrant City, Alabama, where my dad was coach. He had coached at one other place, Brookwood High School in Tuscaloosa County, where he met and married my mother in the last part of her senior year. Soon after their marriage, my dad joined

7

the navy at the beginning of World War II and served as a physical trainer until the end of the war.

Life for us was about to become supercharged. One morning I saw a Mayflower moving-company van outside our small apartment in Tarrant. We were moving to Attalla, Alabama, where Jim Glover would begin coaching the Etowah Blue Devils. The year was 1947.

My dad coached the Blue Devils for thirty-three years to culminate with his induction into the Alabama Sports Hall of Fame. His very first season there was fabulous—his football team was undefeated, and he coached the basketball team to the state championship. There were few losses at Etowah in those early years.

My father's greatest fame in coaching came from the trick plays that he used against some of the strongest teams in the South. He was especially known for his water bucket play, which was actually used in the 2006 season by Arkansas. That type of football play had another name used by some that I will not mention now for the sake of correctness. The key point here is that this was his style—deception, not power or perfection of technique. It is quite possible that I learned this style of deception too well.

To draw some conclusion to this topic—roots—our family was pretty poor during most of our years at home. My father once sent my mother to the old Guy Kelley Auto Auction to sell our only car while he conducted football practice. After losing our car, we walked.

From my viewpoint now, it seems that the apples do not fall very far from the tree. I seem to have taken traits from both parents. From my father, I have taken some of his creative ability; he was a great innovator and even a poet. He also liked to work in fun things like football, and not manual things like the soil. The same goes for me. From my mother, who was gentle, compromising, and musical, I have taken my gentleness and my non-confrontational style, but not the music. I do love music. (Once in the ninth grade, I even asked my mother to let me join the high school band as a drummer. She put that thought down pretty quickly.) To be honest, as much as I love football, I never liked hitting people or being hit. With this said, when my buddy, Bobby Payne who played at Auburn, was asked whom he thought the toughest player on our team was, he stated, "Jerry." I guess compromise came easy.

Times were tough for my brother Neil, my mother, and me. Later, a younger brother came along when things financially were maybe better. I say more about this in the next chapter.

5

Programmed to Fail

My brother Neil, who is eighteen months younger than me, made a statement recently that explains much about the realities in both of our lives. The statement was, "We were just programmed to fail."

The full reality of this is that every human, without properly responding to God's plan for all mankind, is programmed to fail. God is real. Heaven is real, and hell is real. Our response to these truths determines whether we are winners or losers. The winners are those who choose correctly, and they win big—I mean big. The losers, even though they are here on Earth and may look good, will eventually become Coach Townsel's "look-good losers." While in college at the University of Alabama, where I had received a scholarship as football manager under Coach Paul Bryant, the very worst thing one could say about a person was that he was a loser. Well, that was my outcome—at least until the coffee shop experience on June 2, 1987, that is.

Our program for failure actually began with our inherited eye defect, which is passed to male children through the mother. My grandfather suffered from this, as well as my brother and male cousins. We had a condition, which some call lazy eye, that also carried with it extreme farsightedness. We are just shy of being legally blind. Adding to this problem were my crooked teeth, thin hair, skinniness, and the biggest obstacle of all, poor self-esteem caused by a lack of proper parental nurturing. In no way do I blame my parents for this lack of nurturing, because they had their own problems in this very area, especially my dad. My father is known as a powerful positive example and father figure to probably thousands of boys and young men, but it's just a fact: his own boys were not properly nurtured or taught. To make sure this is not taken wrongly, I worshipped my father and loved my mother, and I owe them all that I am. I can tell anyone with certainty that my father, who is now in heaven, approves of what I've said. The ending is what counts, not the beginning. As Coach Bryant taught, "It's the fourth quarter that we must win. The fourth quarter is ours. It ain't over till it's over."

Because of those conditions early in life, I learned to fantasize about being another person whom I saw as being okay. I even learned to be a deceiver by speaking out about that imaginary person, hoping people would believe this persona. I wanted so much to be accepted and maybe even respected.

At some points in my life one might have looked at my life and said that I was an overcomer, maybe even an overachiever. I was elected to be one of the captains of our high school football team, and I graduated from Alabama and even completed a master's degree. After college I attempted to follow the two men whom I admired most, my father and Coach Bryant, to coach football. For seven years I struggled at this, but finally my compulsive, overaggressive nature caused me to throw in the towel. I could win the battle, but lose the war.

I then found something for which I was better suited—the fund-raising industry. This new endeavor allowed me to earn much more money than any of our family members had ever earned. This endeavor even developed into the formation of my own company, Promar, which grew to be one of the top ten of its type in America. We had grown to have as many as 125 employees before my risk-taking, overly aggressive nature caused another failure after nine years of growth and seeming success.

It is pretty obvious to me now that failure was certain. It was just a matter of time. The limited skills that I had, plus the deceptive tactics upon which I had relied, could take me only so far. That other element working inside me and against me would inevitably dominate my reality.

It was the realization of the upcoming failure that brought me to the point of decision, the point of turning. After all, the worst thing that could be said of someone was that he was a loser. I can remember sitting in church in our town of Albertville, Alabama, one Sunday and thinking about how tough it would be to go bankrupt in that town and in that church. It appeared to me that there was a big stigma there concerning money and the appearance of success. This naturally resembled in my mind the stigma of being a loser in football at Alabama.

Horror of horrors, it was here. There was no ducking out, no more tricks. It would happen. Maybe I might have thought during my time in the coffee shop that a change to Jesus might enable me to avoid the big hit of loosing my beloved company, but I'm not sure. What did occur was that we then entered into the most traumatic times we could have imagined. Now, however, we had an ace in the hole; we had power to endure. The most embarrassing secrets of a deceitful life were revealed, but there was another power now to see me through—the Lord Jesus Christ, the Son of God.

I must say this here: My thoughts about going bankrupt in Albertville, Alabama, and in that church were incorrect. We lived there for over nineteen years after the bankruptcy and experienced real love and understanding. I was just wrong about one more thing.

6

Bubba

In one of my several endeavors since my company Promar failed, I attempted to become a preacher in one of the denominations where the larger church pastors wear robes. Could you picture Jim Glover's son wearing a robe? Anyway, a joke was going around in our training course that went like this: "What were the redneck's last words?" The answer was, "Hey, Bubba, watch this." Many prospective preachers thought this to be funny. It wasn't funny to me. The reason was that it hurt too much for I knew that I had been, and to a degree still was, a Bubba. You may as well know this now: I do not believe that an initial acceptance of Jesus changes anything physical or soulish, except maybe a few miraculous changes, such as my alcohol and my depression. The big deal at your conversion is that you now have a new Spirit working within you. This is not a repaired Spirit or improved Spirit. What you have is a *new* Spirit, the Holy Spirit of God. I was a born again Bubba.

The heart of the Bubba story is this: The redneck says, "Hey, look at me. Look at what I can do. I want you to see me." Very often in my life I had done and said things designed to draw the focus to me, get attention, maybe have my father say something good about me (like he did about those Blue Devils whom I had desired to imitate). I wonder how often this occurs in life. It sure seems very likely that it occurs in the lives of those learning disabled kids who I had attempted to teach after the business collapse. I believe that everyone needs and deserves this attention. I'd bet that the lack of this attention and early nurturing is the basic cause of the serious addiction problems today. These addicted people just duck out of their reality to another reality, a chemical reality.

7

Change

Readers of my generation will probably identify with the things I explain here. The topic is the vast cultural change in American life over the past sixty or so years, a change that I see as disturbing.

Immediately following the big war, Attalla, Alabama, may not have been the very example of American life in general, but back then almost all places and people looked very similar. What I remember most is that things were pretty simple there. There was no visible rush, there were no airs of sophistication, and most of all there was little grabbing for money. Maybe the lack of money-grabbing resulted from nobody having very much of it. You could say that people were much more authentic than those of today. "Mayberry everywhere" would be one way to describe this.

The decade of the fifties was a quiet time with the main focus on Communism and the nuclear threat from Russia. This was the time when I was attending elementary school and junior high. One big thing did occur—rock music, including Elvis and the Beatles—but the big, big changes were coming very soon in the sixties.

As I moved from peaceful Attalla of the fifties into the sixties in Tuscaloosa at the University of Alabama, some mighty and significant events unfolded, events that changed our nation big-time. In my first year of college we traveled back to school on Sunday nights from home. As we passed through Birmingham at night we often saw smoke from fires and black people standing on the dark street corners. We even sat on the street curb across from the Etowah County Courthouse and watched as the demonstrators were dispersed very forcefully. I saw the new convertible auto of a black musical group slashed and doused with paint at a fraternity party once. There was much more of this, and looking back, surprisingly, it all seemed normal and okay. It was just the way things were. That's it, just the way things were.

Two black students enrolled at the university in the beginning of my first years there. That was the year when George Wallace stood in the schoolhouse door also. The state militia operated from our football field house and lived in our dorm. There was also a guy named Martin Luther King who was always on TV, and there was a big mess one day at a bridge in Selma, Alabama.

Another big change, the biggest of all, was developing in a place we had never heard of: Vietnam. While still in college, I learned that one of my best buddies and a teammate from Etowah, Auburn Foreman, was killed there in an accidental strafing from our own air force. Other friends would die there also.

At Alabama, panty raids and beer bashes were big things, especially with the fraternity boys. The drug of choice was Dexedrine; it allowed us to stay up late to study prior to exams. I knew of no one who had any chemical addictions. There was a lot of what we called then, *cussin;* I was pretty good at it, but not as good as Coach Bryant. Coach Bryant was very good at using strong language to get our attention. This point was made my very first day at the field house. An older student manager informed me that while I watched the gate for unwelcome visitors, I was not to make any slipups. He said, "You don't want Coach Bryant on your case. You've never been cussed out like he will cuss you out." I discovered this personally in the following years; it even brings out a story or two that I will share later.

Looking back now, here are a few of the changes that I observed. As far as I could determine, church was a nice place to go, we went almost every Sunday but very few people around me seemed to take it seriously. In fact, my father, while sitting in the back row, would work on his football plays almost every week. I had only met a few people, including Steve Sloan, our great quarterback in 1965, and Richard Cole, who seemed to be serious about Jesus Christ. Divorces were almost unheard of. Homosexuality was so rare that everyone knew of the two or three gay people in town. Often these people received abuse, especially from the guys at our athletic dorm.

Cheating on tests was almost essential for those of us who were not very concerned about learning, but just wanted to get by. This was, however, a very costly mistake on my part.

I can remember how my first roommate, Jimmy Davis (now Dr. James Davis), stayed up late with his lamp burning, studying, studying, studying. He is now an orthopedic surgeon; then he was a student athletic trainer. There were others, of course, who studied, like Dr. Gaylon McCullough, but there was also "Hoot Owl," my second roommate and the person whom I followed to become the head manager. Hoot Owl was a powerful shaper of my life until the day he was dismissed from his job as head manager. This was at the same time that Joe Namath was suspended from the team. Had I not gone to Attalla that weekend I may well have met the same fate.

Of all the changes, the biggest one I have observed is the change from the authentic earthiness of people to the superficial, robotic plasticity of men in our current society. People in those days were real—you got what you saw. I must inject here that, as I noted earlier, I was an entrepreneur type, maybe even ahead of my time. I was perhaps the first superficial plastic man. I just didn't think people would offer me very much if they saw the real me.

I recently attended a graduation function in which my youngest son Chad received his MBA with honors from a very good private university. Let me put things this way: This crowd was tight; it made me tight. The kind of talk there would have been laughed at severely around the football office, field house, and athletic dorm in Tuscaloosa. This talk would have placed the people of Attalla into shock. How Chad was able to cope so well in this tight environment is beyond me. I just wonder how much further things can go in this direction. I'm seeking real people with whom to be friends and brothers. I need them, but how can you know who the real really are today?

While the religious environment of the fifties and sixties may not have been a very dominant factor in our lives, there's one thing that can be said for it. That one thing is that there was little pretense about it, few religious masks. We're very deep now into pretense and masks today. I've seen only one way by which we can know the real from the fake. The real ones come unto obedience to Christ's second commandment of His new covenant. That command is that we love all our brothers who are in Him, not just those in our denomination or church.

While religion is much more prominent today in American lives, more discussed, and even maybe more important, the overall integrity of life has definitely declined. It looks to me as though there are more professors today than possessors. One key reason that I make this assessment is that I just never seem to hear anyone talking about Jesus. It seems to me that if we really possessed Him, then we'd just have to talk about Him.

I sincerely believe that those who truly seek to follow Jesus today are more dedicated than those in the years that I mentioned earlier. The big difference is that there are also more fence-sitters now than before. Possibly you could say that all three of the possible groups have become more focused. The real believers are definitely more focused. Those fence-sitters, or what the Bible calls the "double-minded" or "wavering," have increased their visibility and numbers greatly. Some of these are even called Evangelicals today because they work so aggressively to spread their own religious views. The third possible group is the one that has changed the most. This group contains the non-believing, non-church-attending ones, and even the anti-church group, which is extremely active and visible today. This would have been a dangerous stance to take publicly forty years ago.

We recently kept two of our four grandchildren for one week. My grandmother had a saying: "Pretty is as pretty does." Raising children is currently an undertaking that can put you very near to being in an out-of-control condition. My grandkids are wonderful, but how can one live a life of his own today, devote as much time to kids as seems to be the standard, and keep one's sanity? Raising children is a very big area of change today. Another saying of yesteryear is, "Children should be seen, not heard." Far, far away are we today from those times. There may have been some balance in the days when our kids were young, but now there is no balance at all.

It's going to be painfully proven one day that this method of child-rearing does not work, but today we're being held hostage to unsound logic and political correctness. *Sparing the rod* and *time-out* are sheer madness. We seem unable today to balance ourselves in almost any manner. Liberalism is totally absurd. Conservatism is too oppressive. But there is no balance. We can't even allow the upright parents to properly discipline their children because of all the deviants and psychos who abuse their own children. So, what happens? We all fall off a cliff. Much of our change has now been allowed enough time to mature, and the fruit that has been produced is very bitter.

8

The Blue Devils

The success that my father, Jim Glover, experienced in Attalla, Alabama, can be described as early, phenomenal, and continual. Truly, Jim Glover and Etowah High in Attalla were a match that would be deep and stay long. I mentioned his early success in both football and basketball, but there were also baseball and youth sports. Jim Glover was a coach. He loved it and pretty much lived it.

The Blue Devils grew to such widespread fame and notoriety that in the late fifties and early sixties it became difficult to schedule games. Etowah was not a big school, with maybe seven hundred to eight hundred students in the top three grades. But this little school was able to compete successfully with some of the largest schools in the state and even out of state. Schools from Tennessee and Mississippi were regular opponents, and I really can't remember an out-of-state team ever defeating the Blue Devils.

My father's success can be best divided into three areas. First, he was a motivator of the first degree. His pre game talks would bring tears, and the attitudes of players there were just as positive about winning as those of the Alabama program. We just expected to win. It didn't matter how things may have looked on the scoreboard; the Blue Devils could come through to victory and did on many occasions. I can remember very well one game, a road trip. The Blue Devils scheduled the famed Black Bears of Tuscaloosa. There was so much fan interest that a complete train was chartered. The band, the team, the cheerleaders, and dozens of fans traveled by train to Tuscaloosa, where they were participants in a parade through the downtown streets. The Blue Devils came home with another victory.

Second, Gentleman Jim (as some people in the media called him) possessed creativity, which certainly led to his success. He could see weaknesses in the opponent that could be exploited. He also knew which strings to pull to keep the momentum alive. I can still see him now, sitting in his old recliner drawing up plays and making plans.

Third, he understood extremely well that in order to compete well in athletics, one needs athletes very badly. Recruiting both within his school and outside of it was a constant pursuit. His biggest school rival, Gadsden, had been able to bring a big guy named Terrell Wallen there to play in the late fifties. Gadsden had stolen him from Chattanooga Central that very same year. His picture remained in the Central football program the entire season. Actually, Central had brought Terrell in from Trenton, Georgia, where he was too old to compete his senior year. The following winter, my dad and his buddy, James Kilgo, decided to travel up to Trenton to see if there were other big kids like Terrell up there. They went to the Trenton, Georgia, head coach, who directed them to one such boy. In selling the boy about the benefits of being a Blue Devil, they asked him, "How old are you?" His response was, "How old do you want me to be?"

My father may not have been the best coach, but he made more noise and drew more attention than the normal coach. He was the first proponent for a football playoff system, and he even had some friends in the state legislature introduce a legislative motion for that purpose. As I mentioned earlier, he was one of the very few high school coaches to be inducted into the illustrious Alabama Sports Hall of Fame.

During his tenure at Etowah, he was given several automobiles, the first of which was the 1952 Chevy given to him when we were forced to sell our only car. The last vehicle was awarded to him at Jim Glover Day in Attalla to celebrate his retirement.

Being a Blue Devil was a big deal and the coach was the biggest deal. Jim Glover was exciting and likeable and even humble to a degree. He did like his attention, but he never forgot his roots in the soil of Moundville.

9

This Is Alabama Football

All the remaining team members from the 1964 National Championship Team had been invited to the opening football game of the 2004 season for the forty-year reunion. At the final event of the reunion, the team members were introduced to the crowd of over 82,000 at halftime. After completing the introduction, the public address announcer said very powerfully, "This is Alabama football." At hearing this, a wave of goose bumps went from my legs through my entire body. This is Alabama football. This meant that excellence and winning championships is what Alabama football is about. Winning was familiar to me even prior to coming to Tuscaloosa. The Blue Devils had established a very similar reputation at the high school level, but winning at Alabama had taken this to another degree.

Let me describe my four years at Tuscaloosa. The fall of 1962 through the spring of 1966 could best be stated as being four years of football Camelot. My years there were not the only Camelot years. Since Coach Bryant had come back home to coach there, one national championship had already been won in 1961. It was exciting, to say the very least, and it was definitely life-changing. It made a mighty impact upon my own eighteen-year-old horizons and expectations. Winning and losing were emblazoned into my psyche: You were either a winner or a loser. The big factor determining whether you were a winner or a loser was class. Coach Bryant always told us, "You have class. Class tells." Class seemingly came from paying the price—doing things the right way, not the easy way. My problem was that the thing that was working inside me kept saying, "You can't compete in this way. You'll never win like that."

In these years I had the privilege of brushing up against—not touching, but definitely brushing up against—greatness. Greatness was a person:

21

Coach Paul Bear Bryant (and all the other greats who were assembled around him). How's this for a who's who of coaches: Gene Stallings, Howard Schnellenberger, Pat Dye, Ken Meyer, Charley Pell, Jimmy Sharpe, Pat James, Clem Gryska, Mal Moore, Ken Donahue, Richard Williamson, and others. I'd bet that there's never been a better coaching staff assembled together anywhere.

There were other equally great players: Lee Roy Jordan, Bill Battle, Joe Namath, Steve Sloan, Ray Perkins, and Kenny "Snake" Stabler, just to name a few. Using the word "excellence" is in no way exaggerating the athletic performance of these guys. Most of these guys were class acts off the field also. Lee Roy had, and still has, class. Steve Sloan does also. What was it about these two men that could be called "classy" in the midst of possibly a very tempting opportunity to get spoiled? I'd bet you could look back to their homes and get some answers to this. They had great abilities and talents, but their class came from another area.

As I said earlier, everything centered on Coach Bryant. Coach Bryant came to Alabama in 1957 to restore the football program. The state of Alabama—even the Auburn people—changed then forever. Down South, especially here in Alabama, our identity and state of well-being was attached to how well our team succeeded. To a degree, we were winners if our team won, losers if it lost. That's good, I guess, on a simple level, but things in life really get much more complicated than that.

Now, back to my experience as a student manager. As a student manager, even the head student manager who had keys to almost everything on campus, I was sort of an on-the-wall guy. I wasn't a coach or a player; however, I probably had more contact with Coach Bryant than most of the others. At that time, there was no adult equipment manager on payroll; I was it. I had the only key to the equipment room. I could buy equipment when needed and was in charge of the teams getting to the movie on Friday night and onto the bus on Saturday. I even stood right beside Coach Bryant on the sidelines at the games. I called the players who would go into the game as Coach Bryant gave me their names. When we boarded the plane or bus, the players wore crimson blazers, and I wore a suit. When the team was introduced at pep rallies, I stayed back in the seats.

Well, from whatever the vantage point, I was there. I saw strong images and heard stories and formed some strong opinions from that which I observed. At the center of it was, of course, Coach Bryant, whose 6'2" or more stature, gruff voice, and aloof but also intimidating demeanor certainly demanded the attention and respect of all involved. It's hard to describe someone who is almost more than life, but that's how he was. I've never known anyone else like him. It's going to be interesting here in Alabama to see if our new coach, Nick Saban, will be able to keep the media wolves at bay as Coach Bryant was able to do.

Today, this aggressive treatment from the media has been tolerated, but it has affected every coach since Coach Bryant. The old saying, "It would be better to bear the cross than to cross the bear," is true as far as I can tell. I have seen very few people crossing him, not even the media. It looks as though Coach Saban has read the book, and I'd bet on him keeping things workable.

In my first year at Tuscaloosa, I don't think Coach Bryant ever spoke a word to me, which was just fine with me. He might have asked me to go across the street to Art's Char House to get him a couple packs of Chesterfields or something like that, but nothing of any substance. My second year was moving along smoothly as well until the week in which President Kennedy was killed. His assassination caused our game in Miami with the University of Miami to be postponed. We were then given two or three days off from practice, and a few of us spent one afternoon cruising and drinking a few beers. After returning from the outing, as I was taking a hot shower in our brand new Bryant Hall athletic dorm, my buddy Tim, who had been out with us, threw an entire garbage can full of cold water on me. As this cold water was hitting my body I let out a loud G.D., the first one I can remember ever saying. As I walked out into the hall with no shower shoes on and no robe, which were also no-no's, Coach Bryant was standing right there, right in front of the shower room. What he said was short: "See me in the morning," which meant before breakfast, that is, if you could eat any breakfast that morning anyway.

As I knocked on his door at the coach's office around 6:15 AM, he said gruffly, "Come in." I walked across his big office to his desk and said, "You asked me to come over." His response was, "If this ever happens again your ass is gone." Well, this caused me to fall from grace and lose a later trip to the Miami game. It also cost me a Sugar Bowl watch and postponed my being made head manager for a month or so. The vacancy for head manager occurred when my roommate Hoot Owl was dismissed as head manager after a night out with Joe Willie Namath. Coach Bryant called them in on Monday morning. An interim head manager, who helped us some but was really a very good baseball player, was named in my place. Once the Sugar Bowl was over, I took over as head manager for the remaining two and a half years at Alabama.

There's another story about an early morning visit to Coach Bryant's office, which I share in the next chapter. In this story the tables were turned, but I ended up being the dunce anyway.

10

Other Stories from Inside the Camp

I'd love to be able to write another book on the four years in Camelot. Life was exciting there, but there was one thing you did not want to occur, to not be aware of where Coach Bryant was located. Someone once said that an offensive coach or quarterback should know at least one thing: where Cornelius Benett, the great linebacker, is located. I didn't know where Coach Bryant was that day in the shower, and it cost me.

I can hear Coach's voice now, "Manager!" When we heard that, our response was to immediately jump, execute a half circle to determine where he was located, and then sprint to that place. This even happened once while I was attending a practice four years after my graduation, while I was coaching at Moundville. He called out, "Manager!" and I jumped. He would call me Jerry in private.

One story, which is known by no one but me, involved that swearing deal, or actually part two of it. We had opened the season by losing to Georgia by the famous flea-flicker play in my senior year of 1965. Ole Miss was coming up next, and things were getting tight at practice.

We always knew that as long as Coach Bryant stayed on his tower, things were at least not critical. However, on the Tuesday before Ole Miss, Coach Bryant came down from the tower cussing and ripping.

In August, we were on the field one morning in the normal closing circle when Coach announced that there had been a newly formed fellowship of Christian athletes and all cussing and swearing fines would go to it. It was my duty to assess the fines. Fines were: for the players—fifty cents, the assistant coaches—one dollar, and the head coach—ten dollars. It was a task that I very much turned a deaf ear to because it was trouble.

Now, back to the Tuesday practice, which had gotten very hairy after Coach came down from the tower. After practice, Coach Bryant came to the window of the equipment room and told me that he probably owed me some money for swearing. Well, I bopped right over to his office the next morning at about 6:15 again. I knocked again on his door and was greeted with, "Come in." As I walked again across the office and approached his desk, I noticed a shoebox on the floor, and placed toe-to-toe on his desk was a new pair of alligator shoes. I said, "Coach, you asked me to come over." He replied, "How many times did I swear?" Very foolishly I responded, "Five times," which was probably too few, but I should have said once. He gave me a look that I can't forget, and then as he was making out a check for fifty dollars I made another mistake. I asked him, "Does this go to the FCA?" His response was, "Hell, no, give it to Coach Laslie." I'm pretty sure Coach Laslie knew what to do with it. The shoes on his desk proved, I suppose, that he really was a real human being after all, I'm sure we all have a little vanity.

One other story may amuse some readers. In the national championship season of 1965, which was my last season following a national championship in 1964, we had several unusual events occur around the managerial staff. The 1964 season had gone pretty smoothly for me, but things got a little wacky in 1965, starting with the aforementioned swearing event. We had lost our first game to Georgia in Athens, and then we started getting on track until the bizarre ending of the big rival game in Birmingham against Tennessee. We were tied 10–10 with only a few seconds left on the clock. We had the ball in easy field goal range, maybe the ten-year line of Tennessee. Coach Bryant sent Snake (Kenny Stabler) into the game to hold for the field goal try, but Snake, mistakenly thinking it was third down, threw the ball to the ground to stop the clock. That ended the game. More excitement was about to occur. The passageway for players at the old Legion Field was narrow in those days. As I proceeded into this passageway the players backed up and stopped. Coach Bryant impatiently asked, "What's wrong?" Someone said, "The door is locked."

This door being locked denoted a very serious mistake made by some manager. Coach Bryant, while walking up to the rickety old door, said, "Knock the son of a b**** down." He then proceeded to do so with his right forearm, which we called in football terms "the flipper." My helper, Jim Bowman, had gotten caught up with the ending of the game and had forgotten to unlock the door. Things could have gotten ugly for us, but luck was with the managers that day.

After lunch the following day, Coach Laslie came over to the field house and wanted me to walk over the practice fields with him to check for places that needed watering. After a few minutes, he said calmly, "Jerry, don't let that happen again about the door." Paul almost broke his arm.

Jim Bowman wasn't through after forgetting the door. On the next Tuesday, Coach Bryant came to the equipment room window again and told me that we were not to go to the other team's dressing room to retrieve the game ball, especially when the game ended in a tie. I never knew this until that moment, but Jim had gone into the Tennessee dressing room and, in the presence of the Tennessee media, had asked the head coach for the game ball.

We made one other boo-boo later that year. We were playing Mississippi State at their new stadium in Jackson. At that time, Mississippi State used a football with a different feel than that of our Wilson TD. When we played on the road and used another type of ball, we would practice that week exclusively with the other team's type of ball. As the equipment truck was loaded for the trip to Jackson, someone slipped up and put our Wilson TDs on the truck and no Spalding J5Vs.

About five minutes before we were to go out for pregame warm-up, one of my helpers came to me with the news about the balls. I panicked, as I should have. I then fessed up to Coach Laslie, who then went to Coach Bryant. The team was dressed and seated prior to going onto the field at this time. Coach Bryant responded calmly, "Come on, Jerry." He and I then went under the stadium to the state dressing room. Coach Bryant knocked on the door and asked their manager if he could speak to their head coach Paul Davis. Coach Bryant explained the problem and asked to borrow a few J5Vs and Coach Davis calmly agreed. The Mississippi State team was in the midst of some pregame talk then also. I dodged a big one that night. I received grace.

We lived through all this and went on to win a second consecutive national championship, allowing me to receive my second national championship ring. Usually the senior players, especially the good ones, would be awarded a local day in their town or city at which time they would receive a new car or such. Well, can you believe this? My town, Attalla, along with the neighboring city of Gadsden, created a Glover-White Day to honor two University of Alabama head managers. Gary White probably deserved it. He had been head manager of the 1961 national champions and was the dorm director in 1965. He was totally dedicated and loyal, but for me this went too far. I believe that the whole atmosphere of the two championships was the big reason for this event. Coach Bryant and the eight or ten senior players who had survived four years were the real honorees.

11

More from the Capstone

When my mother dropped me off at the athletic office in late August 1962, it didn't take very long for my eyes to open to the seriousness of my new life. As I mentioned in another chapter, I had been warned about messing up. I was told that Coach Bryant would "get you." My very first duty was to stand at the only gate on our practice field to check passes. Not knowing anyone in town, I did as I was told and checked passes. One mature-looking, well-dressed young guy came up, and I asked him for his pass. His reply shook me. "Freshman," he said, "you'll regret this. I'm Charlie Pell." Of course, I recognized the name Charlie Pell as a starting tackle from the previous year's national championship team. Once he had put on his uniform for practice he came back out to the gate just to remind me who he was.

Within a couple of days, the freshman players all reported to and assembled in the basement classroom of the coach's office. There were about thirty-six guys there for the first meeting; only about ten finished their eligibility in 1966 with our second national championship.

This will seem hard for some people to believe, but many of the better athletes in that room never put on a jersey in their second year. There were guys like Wayne Treece, Carl Fields, and Phil Dabbs as linemen. The best-looking quarterback prospect was not Steve Sloan, but Jim Tom Oliver. We had running backs such as Charles Crysel, Bobby Baggett, and Larry Lackey. Steve Bowman wore a green jersey for the third team. Jerry Duncan was so far down the line even I, the manager, didn't know much about him. The guys who made it through, over the proverbial obstacle course wall, went on to win back-to-back national championships.

By the year 1962, Coach Bryant had been at Alabama long enough to establish his program. His team even won a national championship in 1961. The stories that I heard from the early years in the late 1950s were pretty bizarre. I heard these stories from some of those who were there. One story was about two players who were at practice one day in the back of a line, waiting to take their part in a drill. One player said to the other, "Let's get out of here." The other player's response was, "No, we can't. That gate is locked and that is an 8-foot fence." Pretty soon there was the noise of a clanging fence—the first player was scaling it.

Coach Bryant had inherited a program in disarray. The quality of the player talent and the conditions were terrible. It was generally understood that the measures for training in those early days were extremely demanding. The mode of personal survival was the only option; only the most gritty alley fighters could survive. By the time of the 1962 freshman class, we had players of pretty high standards. These guys would prove to be tough, but not street fighters.

There had been a well-publicized incident in Birmingham at the Georgia Tech game in 1961, before I came to Alabama. It involved one Alabama player, Darwin Holt, and a Tech player, Chick Granning. There was some bad blood brewing in Atlanta toward Alabama because of this incident. When we arrived in Atlanta in 1962 for our game with Tech, we were greeted and treated harshly. It was dangerous that day to be even a manager on the sidelines that day because whiskey bottles were flying. We lost the game that day and also the sideline whisky bottle barrage.

In 1963, Tech came back to Birmingham, we defeated them, and everything seemed to have calmed down. The next year, Joe Namath's senior year, we went back to Atlanta. Before going onto the field for pregame warm-ups, Coach Bryant came to me and said that he wanted a helmet that would fit him. He tried a couple and finally found his size. He then put on the helmet and wore it onto the field for warm-ups. We won the game that day also. Namath bombed them with a couple of aerial bombs. He only played sparingly that day because his knee had already been injured.

I have several memories of Joe Namath. The first is at the hospitality house, where our only TV was located. On Sundays we would go over there to watch pro football. I can remember Joe yelling in his Pennsylvania dialect, "Roll Colts." It was the Colts that his Jets defeated in the first AFC Super Bowl win.

Only the managers could know another story about Joe. It was our job at practice to have a football ready at the line of scrimmage when the team broke the huddle. There was no tolerance for the lack of a football being a time delayer. Joe would accept only new footballs, because they had a different feel than older ones. At one practice on a Monday night, I had mistakenly placed an older ball at the line of scrimmage. As the team broke the huddle, Joe spotted the ball, ran to it, and threw it over the fence. Coach Schnellenberger was in charge of that drill and was the very last, apart from Coach Bryant, you would want to be there when you were without a football. He had a powerful voice, "Manager, manager, get us a blankety, blank football." Joe got me that night.

As a sophomore manager, I would go out early to set up the field with dummies, scrimmage vests, balls, and so forth. Joe would come out early to warm up, and he would say, "Jerry, let's go." We stood ten years apart—me a half-blind, clumsy guy and Joe Namath with a new pointed-nosed football. He would throw bullets at me and my arms would have knots, but I never let on about this. We also had a little joke between us. Joe had huge hands with long fingers, and I had small hands with short fingers. When I would be standing behind the huddle at a drill he would chide me to play with him by pulling the ball away. He could pull the ball from my hand at will.

When Alabama played Texas in the Orange Bowl, Joe received his $400,000 contract to go to the AFL New York Jets. Back in the hotel someone said something to Joe about his needing to comply with some request of our head trainer, Jim Goosetree. Joe's response to this was, "Goose is just a friend now!" It seemed that many of my remembrances involve Joe Namath; he was certainly a colorful person. Another story involves Joe only indirectly. As you may recall from another chapter, Coach Bryant had suspended Joe for the balance of the 1963 season, along with head manager Hoot Owl Hicks. We played without Joe in the Sugar Bowl, with Steve Sloan as quarterback. We kicked four Tim Davis field goals to beat Ole Miss that day. Upon leaving the field with the game ball, I was met by Hoot Owl just outside the dressing room door. Hoot Owl asked me to give him the Sugar Bowl game ball, and I did.

I recently had sadness. I was calling on schools in Hoot Owl's hometown of West Blockton. I had planned to visit with Jack and talk about old times. I found out that Jack is not doing well now. He has had several strokes and has had a foot removed. Everyone there was anxious to direct me to his house, but as I arrived I found no one home. They said that Jack goes in and out with his ability to communicate. I went back the next day to visit Jack, we had a good visit and I again saw the Sugar Bowl football.

Oh, the stories I could tell about Jack "Hoot Owl" Hicks. I can see him now getting off the team bus, headed into the dressing room and wearing that big Stetson cowboy hat that he had received at a Bluebonnet Bowl trip. He'd say sometimes when he was about to light up a cigar, "Hey, Hoot Owl, have a White Owl."

I can say one thing with certainty: If Coach Bryant was living today, he would visit Jack, and Joe Namath would be there. Joe has always been close friends with Jack. Joe and Coach aren't too concerned about one's station in life. They appreciate loyalty. Jack was loyal.

12

Funerals and Deaths

The years of my life have encompassed many deaths of significant people, including the first notable one for me: President Kennedy. The death of Elvis was significant for me also. My wife, Karen, and I had just attended his concert in Huntsville only a few months before his death. He was the King of entertainers and must have had a very big hearted guy as well.

Within my own personal sphere, three deaths have occurred that have touched me greatly, and the sense of loss from these will never be removed. My mother passed away in February of 2007. She outlived my father by almost twenty years. During the twenty years, I had many opportunities to get very, very close to her in some physically hard times for her. I sometimes kid my brother, Neil, saying that he was really her favorite; of course, this wasn't so. She did spend much time in the doctor's offices and hospitals, and since she lived near us I was the one to go with her most often. I was present, as was Karen, Chad, our youngest son, and his wife Kristy, when she passed away. I'll never forget this and will miss her always.

My father's passing was equally memorable. We were all there, and he just went to sleep very peacefully. As I stated earlier, I was privileged to fellowship with him for seven weeks between my starting a life with Jesus and his death. For me, this time was beautiful. He had a favorite cassette tape by a guy named Squire Parsons. His favorite song on it was "Beulah Land." I would leave my office in Albertville in my silver Mercedes, plug in that tape, and let it play all the way to the hospital in Birmingham, tears flowing all the way. That song went like this; I'm kinda homesick for a country of which I've never known before. My dad was homesick for that very country.

Another death that touched me greatly occurred one afternoon as I was bringing our son, Chris, to the office from his school. As we were stopped at the traffic light beside Weathers Hardware, the radio broadcaster announced the death of Coach Bryant. Over the two-day mourning period, his photo was continuously shown on TV. The state of Alabama and the football world were in mourning, and I was in mourning also.

This is sort of out of character for me, but I decided to go down to Tuscaloosa for his funeral. I got up early and traveled to Tuscaloosa just to be there. When I parked and proceeded to the First Methodist Church where the service would be held, I saw a large number of TV satellite trucks across the street and people located both across the street and behind barriers in front of the church. Someone said that all former players and special funeral attendees were to be in front, and some would be directed into the church later.

As I stood inside the barriers alone, the funeral directors began allowing people to file into the church. The crowd began to climb the steps and then would stop. At one point, the directors came out and said, "We can have only five more come in." They then pointed to two or three and then to me, and we were ushered into the service and told to stand about fifteen feet from the coffin.

Upon walking to my car, I decided to go ahead of the funeral procession and return early to Albertville. As I drove home down the now Paul Bryant Drive, I saw a large crowd of people on the sidewalks similar to those crowds of a parade. The crowds grew as I traveled down McFarland Boulevard. As I entered I-59, I noticed large crowds at every overpass, many with signs. One sign I remember said, "Cottondale Loves You, Bear." I was pretty choked up.

As I drove, I decided that I wanted to pull off the road and see the hearse go by. I wanted one more way to honor this man. I waited a few minutes for the procession to pass—the police, the hearse, the entourage, and the busses with Coach Perkins and the team. I can still see it now.

13

More About "Class Tells"

Coach Bryant's big saying was, "Class tells." He said this to the team, "You have it and it will show." What was this class? What are the characteristics of it? How can it be recognized? And who has it? I think the type of class that Coach spoke can be dealt with easily, at least the qualities that resulted in winning football games. Of course, it was understood that this class should carry over into all of life. Hard work, discipline, a positive attitude, and attention to detail come to mind as some of the basic qualities. Also, striving for excellence was possibly the foremost quality. Competing fairly was just understood, and I never recall any tolerance for cheating or cheap shots.

When these qualities have been realized, there seems to be a positive air generated. This air is not cockiness, but rather confidence—the confidence of knowing down deep that this air has been attained. It is valuable to the person and is held onto tightly. To act in a way unbecoming of this air of class is something to be avoided.

Now to the hard part of explaining this "Class Tells." Some qualities have been mentioned that encompass some attributes of this: hard work, discipline, confidence, etc. But there is something much deeper for some people than these qualities. It is mainly this unusual much deeper factor that I most wish to address.

What makes Lee Roy Jordan, Lee Roy? What made Coach Bryant, Coach Bryant? In my years around Alabama football and my years since that time, I have experienced personally only a few people who could be classified as standing above all others, people who had something more special than even those people who were considered great. It's late in life for me to attain this now, but I know it when I see it, and I have seen it.

35

There is an area of thought that may apply to this class issue. Many of us have what is called a "natural anointing." In the Christian world, an anointing is a special presence from God that accompanies someone and enables that person to be more effective at whatever task the anointing is to be applied. Some have distinct anointings to preach, and the difference in their preaching can definitely be detected. Others may have an anointing to teach, and so on. This thought follows that even apart from their Christian service, people have their own unique natural anointings. These natural anointings explain how our gifts are applied successfully to the area in which we are gifted. Some are anointed chemists, some anointed engineers, and so on. It appears that a person operating within his anointings and gifts may have a certain air about his work.

There is another quality in the lives of the ones who have been identified as those with class. These people use few words, and when they speak, people listen. I've noticed that today this person is extremely rare because there is just so much talk out there now that one must be somewhat forceful to even be heard. What amazes me now is that those who really have very little to offer seem to try to offer the most.

I'll reveal a few names of people who I feel exhibit, or have exhibited, class. These are people who, when you're in their presence, give off something that must be noticed. Coach Bryant, of course, leads the list here, followed by Lee Roy Jordan, Gene Stallings, Steve Sloan, Mal Moore, Clem Gryska, and one whom I only saw a couple of times but heard much about, Pat Trammell. These were a few from Alabama that come to mind. I also met another man and even sat across the table from him at breakfast. He was Coach Bud Wilkinson, the famed Oklahoma Sooner coach who was covering our Orange Bowl game with Nebraska for the TV network. The place at the table was the only one remaining as I came to breakfast, and that seat was beside Coach Bryant. This seat was not usually taken quickly.

To walk with this air of class, one surely must be free of scandal and clouds. There was a brief time when clouds gathered over Coach Bryant, the time when the *Saturday Evening Post* article accused him of fixing a game with Wally Butts, the ex-Georgia coach. A sense of concern could definitely be detected, even from his facial expressions.

A drastic change has occurred in America over the last thirty or so years. Ever since Watergate, we no longer allow secrets to remain concealed. Prior to this time, some pretty big ones were just kept quiet. Now everything is on the table: innuendo, gossip, and accusations. I question whether anyone now can retain the air of class that was available earlier.

I do know one guy who I can honestly say has that air of class. He is a missionary, Mike Clark of Guatemala. Mike lives out of the country now, but once was a prosperous Baptist preacher in Louisiana who gave it all up and now is father to over four hundred orphaned Guatemalan children and has founded dozens of churches. I went to his school and worked there with a team of welders to build a bridge for the kids to cross over a dangerous road on the way to their school. Mike will take a licking and not quit ticking; he has that air, and he will not compromise his integrity just to get big or famous.

It would be nice not to be required to make the following statement for two reasons. First, I hate the reality that requires it, and second, this statement will not make many new friends for me from the ministry. Mike Clark has class, Billy Graham has class, Derrick Price had class, R.T. Kendall has class, and Jacky Beck has class. My current pastor, Chris Hodges, and my ex-pastor, Mike Johnson, have class also. There are more, but where are they? The answer is probably that they are in some obscure little place doing work in complete honesty and integrity. They are not tainted with compromise for the sake of notoriety or the necessity for money.

What else can I say about class? I may not be able to effectively describe it, but I sure know it when I see it. I don't see it from the left or the right, from James Carvell to Ann Coulter. Rush doesn't really have it although he thinks that he does. Neither Donald Trump nor Rosie has any of it at all. We need class very badly today, but it is hard to find.

14

Three Types of People

If I am able to convert to paper just a part of that which I have seen in my Spirit, then this chapter will be very enlightening. The parable of the sower prefaces the teaching. This parable has for years been an intriguing Scripture. I was told that it was the most important parable that we could understand for it contained the vital secrets of how God imparts His word unto those whom He has chosen.

Here's a brief outline of the parable, which is found in Matthew chapter 13, Mark chapter 4, and Luke chapter 8. The sower is God, who is assisted here on Earth by God's chosen servants and from the Bible itself. They dispense true seed with power from above the earth. The people who receive this good seed improperly are called wayside soil, stony soil, and soil that is contaminated with thorns and briars. These impediments cause this soil to be nonproductive. Soil that can receive the seed properly is called the good soil. This good soil will bring forth a good crop, which will increase thirtyfold, sixtyfold, or hundredfold.

All soil receives the same exact seed. The only characteristic that determines the end result is the soil's ability to receive spiritual understanding, which comes through its spiritual ears being operative. Spiritual understanding overrides hardness of soil conditions or briars and thorns. Spiritual understanding overcomes hereditary defects, bad environment, or any other physical impairment.

Let's come back down to Earth again. When I was the head student manager at Alabama, part of my duties were to attend every meeting, either the daily 12:40 PM classroom meetings or those on the field at the close of practice. Coach Bryant dispensed much wisdom at both of those times. About once each year, Coach would explain a theory of life that he had acquired somewhere; it was an explanation of three general personality types. The first type was that person who, upon witnessing an event, did not actually realize or understand what he was witnessing. This person probably had a look on his face of *duh!* The second personality type was the person who perceived that thing that was occurring, but either could not or would not get involved in it as an active player. The third personality type was that person who not only saw the significance of an event, but also placed himself in it as an active player. In essence, this person was the only one to benefit from what was occurring. He was able to shuck off any obstacles and receive the reward.

In addition to Coach Bryant's story, I'd like to add one other to it. This story includes our son Chad, who was placed into the accelerated class in the third grade. Chad's teacher had a cute saying, which our family enjoyed. Her saying, which the students quoted, goes like this, "Good, better, best; never let it rest until good is better and better is best."

Now let me merge these two divergent points. In this twenty-first-century America, we live in a time when these points have been perfected. Man in many ways has become the best; he has seen the possible and become involved. Sadly, we are still able to observe the *duh's* eating their way through life, planning their next activity, and such. We also have examples of those who are borderline between the two. These borderline people are hard to detect because they look so much like the third type. They look so similar except that the fruit that they produce is not of the same quality as that of those who see and get actively involved.

Here's the difference between these personality types. The first two types never fully see the magnitude of the event; their eyes are not fully opened. Those who do see and jump into the event have an ability to see something from within themselves. Once this thing is seen from within, those people can become one with the vision. By becoming one with their vision, these people actually work this new picture into their life's reality—a reality that can then be observed and measured.

In essence, this was when man began to build the Tower of Babel. Man can create whatever he can imagine. This now brings us to the very point of this discussion: There is danger in this concept. The Tower of Babel was not a positive event for mankind. These concepts work against God's plan for men. God does desire that we be productive within His parameters, but man left to himself will make an idol of that which he produces.

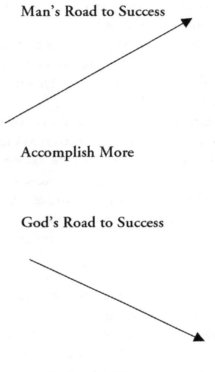

Man's Road to Success

Accomplish More

God's Road to Success

Surrender More

Back now to the parable of the sower. God gives the ability to receive spiritual instruction to those who have spiritual ears. They alone can receive this instruction; they retain this instruction or word into their vision and allow this seed to produce a new reality, a changed man.

Those people who receive the good seed, but without the proper receiving sets, can only produce stale religion, rules, and traditions of men. Those on good soil produce love for God and love for people.

Those people who have no spiritual perception have their minds set only on things such as eating, drinking, and being merry. Their ties are to this world since there is no real perception of the spiritual world.

15

Fatigue Makes Cowards of Us All

The late great Green Bay Packers coach, Vince Lombardi, made two hallmark statements to the entire athletic world. These statements are known throughout the sporting and coaching fraternity. He made the first statement of note at the first Green Bay squad meeting his first year. The team had known very little success prior to his being named coach. The statement, as he stood holding a football in his hands, was, "Gentlemen, this is a football." What Coach Lombardi meant was that nothing would be taken for granted; every aspect of football would be introduced as totally new.

Coach Lombardi's other memorable statement was, "Fatigue makes cowards of us all." Incidentally, there was one other saying that goes like this, "Gentlemen, our priorities here will be: God, family, and the Green Bay Packers." This third statement was so well-known and studied that the late basketball coach, Jim Valvano of North Carolina State fame, used it to address his very first team as a first-year coach at Bucknell. Jim got so carried away when telling his new team about its priorities that he said, "At Bucknell, our priorities will be God, family, and the Green Bay Packers."

There is a message here. Back in my teaching days, I actually became a pretty good reading teacher for kids who needed special help. In the reading world, a functioning reading level called the *independent level* was used to describe the level that we could really function at under pressure. This level would be consistent at any time.

Here is a life finding that I've learned. The difference between the winners and the look-good losers is their level of performance at the independent level. The lesson I've learned is that fatigue of body, mind, or Spirit will cause us to drop down to our independent level. When fatigue comes, we perform at that level only.

Our success at Alabama under Coach Bryant was always heralded in December or January with Bowl games and even two national championships, but the real success started in February in the old gym above the coach's office. Every year from February until spring training, a gym class was held for about forty minutes three times a week. I cannot properly describe the intensity, but I can truly say that I have on several occasions seen three players losing their lunch upon each other above a garbage can in the corner. We once had a non-scholarship transfer from Washington State. This guy was a monster for us. He may have been 6'8" and 290 pounds. Our linemen in those days were about 185 to 190 pounds and 5'10" in height. This big guy lasted no more than fifteen minutes before he was carried to the ambulance by stretcher. In athletics, one performs under stress, in the big games, and especially in the fourth quarter at his independent level. This is the level he will drop down to when his testing comes.

Average people are tested in the same way. We will perform only at the level of our independence. When pressed, we revert down to lower standards. Our real character is only that level which emerges under stress—that's the true us.

Discipline, conditioning, technique, and confidence were key factors at Alabama. These same factors apply in every area of life, even our spiritual life. It's easy to look good when running onto the field. It's still easy to look good in the first and second quarters. True class is the ability to back up your appearance with performance—performance that can maintain itself and operates in a winning manner at its independent level.

16

More About the Real—the Authentic

So far I have made much reference to the topic of realness and reality. In doing this I'm seeking to bring this point to the ultimate dimension—the authentic reality, that which is not a shadow or facsimile. I'm probably an authority on this topic since I'm pretty close to being a past expert on fraud. I've heard it said that it's difficult to con a con. I can speak on this matter somewhat since for five years I worked with a very good ministry called Kairos Prison Ministry. We would go into the state prisons to conduct three-and-a-half-day retreats. We became pretty well-acquainted with the inmates over time and the ways of the cons.

The abbreviation *con* is short for one who has been convicted. That applies well for me. I was convicted, not for a criminal offense, but by public exposure of being a deceiver, a fraud. Looking back I remember how Mrs. Bryant once told someone that Jerry Glover was such a nice boy; Coach had a better perception, I think. By the way, the reason she and I became so familiar was that the seat beside her on our planes was always empty and the last one available. I was always the last person to board, because it was my job to count all players to make sure they made it for the trip. Sometimes Namath was a problem for me since he arrived late very often.

Getting to the real point here, today it is increasingly difficult to determine the real from the fake. It may be easier to tell the less fake from the more fake. Since Promar was dissolved, I have been forced to go into the sale of products, such as furniture. Today, a veneer (or wood cover over particleboard) is considered to be a pretty high-quality product; many products have only a plastic film or picture of wood grain on the surface and particleboard underneath.

Back in the fifties and sixties it was much easier to determine the higher value (the more real) items. When something was advertised back then we could just go in and buy it; bait and switch was unheard of. Truth in advertising back then was not questioned. One could count on the item advertised being of the quality that was stated.

Without any doubt we have now come full circle to the point that most wise people do not trust advertising very much. Overkill or overstatement of quality or price is out of control.

We have talked earlier in this book about what I have called today's robotic plasticity of man. I'd say that these people, while highly sophisticated in technology, are extremely low-tech in humanness and things of their emotions and hearts. Who knows their real feelings or the real person inside?

Today, we're dehumanized in almost every area of life. We can't talk to a real person easily on the phone about our problems, instead we talk to a computer. We're taught about the new way to interact with co-workers, the way to work with the team. The old ways and values must be shelved to allow for the new, better way. Well, it seems to me that this new way is just a pass-the-buck way or move-the-problem-around way. Why can't people respond in a real way?

I have another ax to grind about the new way. The new way for a huge number of people is called the New Age way. There's much more to this New Age way than I can discuss here, but here's the part that brings out the Glover in me. Those New Agers do not deny the reality of the supernatural. In fact, they embrace it wholeheartedly. They believe that there are actual forces at work in the universe, which work miraculously and in supernatural ways. They call these events that occur, events of Karma. Supernatural events could really be from only two possible sources: God or the devil. Which of the two do you think controls Karma? I say that Karma is from the enemy; miracles are from God.

17

Structure Works Against People

Perhaps you have discovered by now my dislike of structure for structure's sake. Rules and order are not the same as structure for structure's sake. Rules and order are necessary and good. Structure for structure's sake is dehumanizing.

As we've grown both in number and in technology, we have a need for both more structure and the means to attain it. Structure is vital in the military, factories, banks, government, and other areas that require mass people-handling. However, structure makes us harder, less tender human beings. Even waiting at traffic lights or waiting in long checkout lines cause stress. Structure entraps us.

My wife, Karen, works in a field that is highly subject to lawsuits. In this field it is almost impossible to just put your arms around someone and tell them the real truth about a situation. Double-talk and legal correctness are vital to avoid lawsuits. Our son, Chris, is a lawyer who practices on the plaintiff's side. He and his senior partner try very hard to avoid frivolous lawsuits. There are, however, more aspiring lawyers in law school today than there are practicing lawyers, and this creates a hunger for clients.

Lawsuits and other legal actions have contributed greatly to the increased need for structure today. There is a true story that I personally enjoy telling about a lawyer who is one after my own heart. It's possible that I may over embellish the story slightly. This lawyer had a client who was overweight, fell from a seat at a McDonald's, and received contusions on her posterior. The lawyer got her his best deal, which I think was a twenty-five-thousand-dollar settlement. Upon hearing her amount, the obese woman became hostile due to her expectation of more money for her condition. In exasperation, the lawyer finally explained to the woman,

"Lady, twenty-five thousand is just what a fat lady gets for contusions on her butt."

Structure is here and we cannot avoid it, but we cannot allow it to harden and dominate us. The very prevalent belief today that the customer must always be right is another strain on our serenity. There is another story that I enjoy telling. It is about an assistant manager of a large supermarket. There was this older lady who gave the checkout workers problems every week and was overzealous to bring merchandise back for refunds. Finally, the assistant manager had taken about all he could take. He told her one day, "Lady, I want you to take your little forty-two-dollar grocery order over to another store." Sometimes we just need to let it out.

People have now become hardened, and many are angry. Who can blame them when all the doom and gloom hits them daily from the media? The TV networks are similar to the story that was told about what Coach Frank Howard of Clemson said about the coach whom he called "Baar." Coach Howard said, "Old Baar can take hissn' and beat yourn, or he can take yourn and beat hissn'." The network can take any side or both sides and beat us down—anything that will attract our attention.

Our frustration and anxiety level is being fed today by our submission to materialistic temptations. Today, we live in homes that we barely can afford; we drive three cars and have boats and lake houses; and we take expensive vacations. We fill our houses with all that fabulous décor (mostly now from China), and our kids must have everything, even the best of everything.

I heard last week on the networks that in America today, 120 million prescriptions for antidepressants were issued last year. The report stated that we were just not happy today. If people will be honest with themselves they may find that their own conditions are very similar to my own condition prior to my company's demise. I saw an imminent collapse on the horizon, and it took only one serious setback to bring it down.

As stated earlier, structure works for things, but it works against people. I suspect that if Coach Bryant had not been such a great communicator, his structure and organization would have been just like those of the others. As for my own needs, I identify with emotions of the heart much more than with principles. If God had not shown me that He personally loved me, then His road maps would have never attracted me.

My best advice for those who have been sucked into this trust of structure, or for those who are caught up in it as is Karen, just look at what it is doing. We may be forced to live with it, but not live for it. We need to see it as it is and for what it will ultimately do. The next step is to move away from the tension and stress, and find one or two people with whom you can be real—people who don't want to see your façade, just you.

Bing Crosby recorded a little song back in 1933 titled "Try A Little Tenderness." At the time of the recording America was in the midst of our Great Depression. We're now right in the midst of our *great inflation*. Why don't we try a little tenderness?

The prophet Joel speaks of a type of army that is marching in lockstep, eating and devouring God's land. According to Joel 1:4, "That which the palmer worm hath left hath the locust eaten, that which the locust have left hath the canker worm eaten, that which the canker worm hath left the caterpillar hath eaten." This devastation is occurring today, and it is devouring our sensitivity. It is taking us captive right within our own bodies and homes.

18

The Holy Spirit Rejects Structure

John 3:8 explains the workings of the Holy Spirit. Jesus stated that the Holy Spirit is likened to the wind: It goes wherever it desires to go. We can hear this wind, but cannot tell from whence it comes or where it will eventually go. The following teaching should be extremely valuable for young believers today.

Apart from the presence of and connection to the Holy Spirit here on Earth, there is no contact with God. Man's initial contact with God involves the wooing of men to God solely by God's Spirit. Past the initial point of conversion, God primarily utilizes the written words contained within the Bible to sustain the believers' need for spiritual food. The words contained within the Bible are God-inspired words that contain spiritual power.

Man's penned words may also contain some spiritual anointing, but not nearly to the degree of those words penned directly from God. The Holy Spirit is very selective concerning how He is represented. He, the Spirit, resists manipulation, presumption, and hype. He is near to those of a sweet, gentle nature.

I've discovered something that could be considered as profound. We as believers contact God through our own old Spirit. Remember, we have a Spirit, a soul, and a body. This Spirit of man, a believer, receives God's Spirit right within the place of our old Spirit, giving us a totally new Spirit, the Holy Spirit. Now, here's the profound part! God's method of contacting man is through His sending spiritual messages to His own receiving stations here on Earth, the indwelling believer. God connects Spirit to Spirit—not Spirit to soul or Spirit to body. The reception methods of these messages from God are: music, the written words from the Bible, words penned from God's anointed messenger, and anointed preaching. That's about all that can be trusted. If it doesn't come by God's man and His method, it is of no value.

Now, how does this apply to life today? As we have grown to be more sophisticated and system-oriented, man has tried to create some new devices and more modern methods from which to receive instruction from God. Today, master sermon writers create messages and distribute them to other less articulate pastors for their own personal delivery. The Holy Spirit resists this type of systemization. These messages sound extremely professional as they really are professionally done. While these messages may impress immature believers, the presence of the Holy Spirit is missing, and nothing of real value exists.

The anointing of God, His spiritual power, is granted to selected vessels. These vessels receive the impulses directly from God; these must come directly to one, not indirectly. Often the Spirit speaks to the person as the person addresses a group. The words are not written down. Other times God gives outlines of key points, and the preacher receives the actual words as he preaches. Formal outlines and written messages do not lend themselves to this.

Here's this lesson in a nutshell: Those who worship God properly worship Him in Spirit and truth. We do not need to hear man's wisdom and are not impressed by articulation or proficiency of delivery. What a spiritual person wants is spiritual food. Spiritual food comes down directly from above, not from UPS or even the local printer with no regard for one's personal charisma or skill of articulation.

If the Holy Spirit inhabits structure, then those guys who light those candles, who spread that fake smoke around, and have all those ritualistic sayings would have the market cornered. The Holy Spirit shuns this stuff like a plague but inhabits the true praise of His people.

We don't learn anything from the Spirit by analytical means. I have a theory. I cannot prove this, of course, but the theory is that the Spirit of man is located in the right hemisphere of man's brain. The left hemisphere is the center of analytical reasoning. I believe the center for love and other emotions are located in the right hemisphere also. This is just my hypothesis. Some people say that the Spirit is down in our heart. My feeling is that the heart is just a pump. Man's heart, his Spirit, is in the right hemisphere. It's okay to disagree with my thoughts on this; this is not very important.

Here's what we must be watchful of: There are good-sounding, well-organized messages that attract people. These come off to the novice as being spiritually inspired, but are only facsimiles of the real thing. I've seen the real thing—you know it once you've seen it. I've seen a midget only 38 inches tall bring the Holy Spirit into a meeting in an awesome way. His strength was his realness. He had no way by which to impress us except through purity. Anointing follows purity very closely. However, anointing, once given by God, can still be retained even in conditions that are not pure. Those preachers who are now concealing willful sins had better watch out, though, because they are being exposed in great numbers today.

19

Courage

At Alabama, we had a great fullback named Steve Bowman. Steve was a very bold guy. I can remember before our national championship-winning game against Nebraska in the 1965 Orange Bowl when Steve made a little talk. In his talk to the team in a closed meeting after lunch the day of the game, Steve said, "If you're scared, say scared." That was just a cliché back then but it speaks to me today.

Fear is not from God; in fact, the Bible says that God did not give us a Spirit of fear (2 Timothy 1:7). It may surprise some of you readers that I admit to being a recovered *fearaholic*. Soon after my conversion, attacks came upon me that caused great fear, even anxiety attacks. I've explained my healing method earlier, that of my determining to face the attack or problem straight on. I've used the example of the obstacle course wall. We may not look pretty while facing this, but we must face it.

The depth of Steve's statement is incredible. If you're scared, just say you're scared, and then suck it up. "Suck it up" was also a big saying at Alabama. "Suck it up" means that if you've got what we called guts and you face obstacles, then you suck those guts up. How many guts does it take to be politically correct? Not many. How many guts does it take to stand up against the norms? A lot. How many guts does it take to be a risk taker, even to follow God in a new direction? More than most people have today.

It requires little courage to get up to fight with one's fists; in fact, this is not real courage at all. Real courage is the inward ability to do the right thing. Coach Bryant,s biggest saying was;" Don't do it the easy way, *do it the right way'.* The right way will cause us to take risky positions, to get out into the deep waters.

Most people who say that they believe in God in reality live as though He does not really exist. Does the Scripture in Romans 8:28 mean anything at all to us? Does God not have an even bigger stake in us than we can conceive? He stands to lose more than we can imagine. The current cookie-cutter systemization cost God His ability to make us into the people we really are supposed to be.

Fear is a force to be feared alright. If not, the devil would not use it so much to control us. Fear, however, is a force to be overcome. It is this overcoming of fear that proves our love for God and our obedience.

20

Two Outdated Words: Authority and Integrity

Modern society has evolved over the years to the position of losing the old meaning of two of our most important benchmarks. Those benchmarks are the submission to authority and the adherence to the highest standards of integrity. This evolution has greatly eroded the very basic elements of honesty and truthfulness in the area of integrity. Submission to authority has been replaced by, *I have my rights; no one is going to tell me what I've got to do.*

A very urgent need for today is our getting back to the point of integrity of word and practice, and getting back to a respect for authority. The new standards of relativism and situational correctness have moved in to take their place. President Clinton even came to to the point of applying his own personal opinion to the meaning of the word "is." The actual or real meaning of the words "integrity" and "authority" neither have nor ever will change. We've changed them to suit our desires for more relaxed and livable standards.

My wife Karen is one of the best doers of Coach Bryant's old saying, "Don't do it the easy way; do it the right way." Coach and Karen both never believed in going cheap or easy. There is no integrity in things that are done improperly or too easily. Cheap merchandise is of little value. This lesson was very difficult for me to accept or apply. Without delving too deeply into this, I saw examples at home of the bending of rules as being okay to do. Sending our spies to watch an opponent practice was looked upon in our house as smart business.

There is a story that I remember to bring this point home; it ended up in detection, but not disaster. Once, Etowah was playing a neighboring school, Alexandria. Two spies were sent on a Wednesday to spy on Alexandria's practice to determine the defensive schemes and trick plays of the opponent. These spies failed to report back on Wednesday. In fact, they came back Saturday morning with a tall tale. While spying on the practice from a tree near the field, the opposing team's quarterback spotted them as he was calling his signals. He notified Coach Lou Scales, who then sent the team in pursuit of the two men to capture them. The two men told my father on Saturday that they were chased down a railroad track by the team. The men dropped dollar bills on the tracks trying to buy time for escape. These men were caught, however, and locked in Alexandria's field house until after the game on Friday night—this story is true.

While at Alabama, I was able to submit to the authority of our coaches because I saw no reason not to do so. They worked hard, had unquestioned knowledge, and competed fairly. Also, these were times when there was not much to observe anywhere as an example of rebellion to authority or even resistance to it. I never recall seeing a man with a ponytail or earrings, tattoo's were mostly on sailors.It was just accepted that those who were placed in leadership were in charge and what they told us to do, we did. It was simple: leaders were installed and we were not installed.

The following story shows an example of the breach of integrity. As I stated earlier, once I left the coaching profession I entered the fund-raising industry with a well-known and respected company. This company name is revered in America as a publisher of magazines, whose appearance of integrity is beyond reproach. I experienced great success with the fund-raising division of that magazine. It was determined that I would switch from my successful territory in northern Alabama to the even more successful territory of a guy who was moving into district management with the company. As a replacement for my territory in Alabama, the competitor to our guy who was moving into management would move to northern Alabama to take my place. My company required this man to call all of his old accounts on the day before I was to go to their school, telling them that he was leaving and that they should switch over to me. By doing this,

his old company had no ability to retain their old business. We made a clean sweep of our only competitor business. Our cunning and trickery stole it all.

This story is just one example of what I've participated in and witnessed in the competitive world of business. At one point, I was given the territory in an industry that contained a very large account in the New Orleans area. The general talk was that my account there, which literally had no competition, was controlled by the Mafia. A story went around that live snakes had once been placed in the office of an upstart competitor. I can't attest to the truthfulness of the above statement, but it's very probable that it is true.

At Promar we never put snakes in the competition's office, but we played very hard. I was told once later that my design man would depict our tiny cheap products in the most deceptive manner of any company in our industry. We also would steal a salesman away from his old employer with little regard for a no-compete contract that he may have signed.

I could fill an entire book with examples of the lack of integrity in business, but the one that really gets to me the most is that of the men of God who fall. I'm now trying to operate on a new system, a system based upon faith in God's word that if I will comply with His ordinances he will take care of my needs. I don't need or want to be deceptive or cheat or lie in this system.

As I attempt to follow this new system based upon faith in God's word, I've found that my conscience convicts me whenever I stray. Believe me, I know about an active conscience; I once lived with a very, very guilty one. I'm still just learning in many areas, but my conscience now works as a proven, safe guide.

Recently, the Birmingham area received news of another respected pastor and evangelist who had been exposed for his twenty-year extramarital affair. This pastor was a man whom I placed at the head of my list for integrity. How could he do it? I'm thankful that God seems now to be screening out the bad apples. This man can ask for forgiveness with a true heart and receive it from God, but I don't want any more leadership from him now. Integrity is at the core of God's plan for mankind, which is why

Jesus never fell into sin. One who is not pure can never purify mankind. If a recent survey is acurate, there are large numbers of pastors in danger. This survey stated that higher than fifty percent of pastors and deacons today admit to visiting a pornographic website at least once per week. Are we not in troubled times if this is accurate?

The meaning of the word "authority" has never been up for reconsideration by God. God has it all: He gives it out to those whom He ordains, such as elected officials, husbands, bosses, and parents. Whether we are right or wrong, when we defy this authority is never debated with God; it is always wrong. We either submit to authority or we reserve our rights; there's no middle ground.

21

The Rod of Correction

This chapter is devoted to the topic of correction and the different approaches to it. I confess that I became dulled and resistant to correction in my early years. *So why,* one might ask, *are you writing about it at all?* The answer is that since correction had not worked well in my life until late, the reasons for its failure in me may help others.

Proverbs 13:24 states: He that spareth his rod hateth his son. "The rod of correction should not be spared. If it is spared then that one hateth his son, but the one who loves his son chastens him." The Bible is the reliable basis for all instruction and can be trusted in its entirety, but not in its exclusivity used to prove just one point. The above Scripture is a very good example of this. To get the fullness of knowledge, we must apply the entire body of knowledge to a matter. In Isaiah 42:3 we see an additional teaching concerning correction. "A bruised reed He, Jesus, will not break and the smoking flax, He shall not quench." This teaching shows that compassion and mercy must be included in dealing with human beings, both children and adults. Jesus does it this way today also.

My early training at home shaped my attitudes and adversely affected my ability to properly receive the positive benefits of correction. My attitude on authority was warped. At our home, we received harsh correction that was sometimes warranted and sometimes not. When my brother Neil needed correction we both got a good dose and vice versa. When it was completed, we were left to alone to recuperate or mend ourselves; no mercy or compassion was ever given.

Now, let's be clear. The same father who operated this way at home was a very effective, fair disciplinarian to his players. I have never heard anything to the contrary, but our home was a different matter. One aspect that led to my not trusting authority figures was that at times discipline was not given out evenly or justly. Sometimes, I took a hit that was needed and other times I took one for the team.

The two men whom I admired most both operated the stick approach; each had a huge carrot also through participating in their football programs. I saw several occasions where Coach Bryant would give money to needy players or buy them a set of tires to make it home. These guys in many cases were not the heroes on the field, not even the good guys, but mercy was shown for mercy's sake. My father had a very big heart also for the little guy.

Throughout life I admit to having had a weakness in the area of respect for authority. This has really hurt at times. It was my perception very early in life that authority figures could not be trusted. Did this have an effect on delaying my decision to accept Jesus Christ as my Lord? It possibly did.

I hope readers will cut me some slack here and indulge me just a little bit while I vent on a matter about which I've stewed for some time now. After all, like the children's song at church, God's still working on me. I have some knowledge that I've acquired, which came about through a very hard-learned personal situation. This lesson fits well into lessons learned about correction and abuse of authority. When my business was forced into bankruptcy, I was in need of a job, something that I could do and be useful at while making a living. I wasn't about to start up any other businesses after the bitter lesson learned there, so I finally reentered education as a learning disability teacher, believing that I would be able to move back into school administration quickly. What ensued was ugly for me. I did return to teaching and received great reward in working with the kids. I may not have been the best teacher, but I was a great kid lover and maybe a good adult role model. Here's the ugly part: I was hired into one of the most political school systems in a whole world of political school systems. Things were done there to keep those at the top in place, and dissent was dealt with harshly.

Now, back from the slack which you've cut me, in special education I saw many kids who had been physically and sexually abused—many. When dealing with those abused kids, I could not use the standard approaches to discipline because the students reacted too harshly. This is an extreme example of the point made earlier: These students' trust in authority was totally gone. They only trusted in themselves. This might have occurred in my life.

God saw something inside me that others couldn't see. What He saw in me was not visible to most people even in the times early on after my acceptance of Jesus. The same thing that He saw in me, He sees in everyone who accepts His call: the ingredients for a humble, teachable Spirit and a contrite heart. He says that He is near such people.

How could the person who was actually abused, and the same person who did not trust authority, ever be brought to the point of accepting real authority and having this gentle, teachable Spirit? I see two possible workings to this. First, this person may have finally come to the big one, the one thing that made all else seem insignificant. The big one for me was that the façade, which I had built for forty-four years, was being exposed and torn down. It was inescapable. This really was the big one. Second, God arranged everything and did it all. He saw something in me that no one else could ever have seen, and He waited for the fruit of it even through some very ugly times. The Bible says that many are called, but few are chosen. God's call goes out even in nature to show Himself; everyone has an equal opportunity to answer this call. I think that in every life there is a time when each person is brought to the point of decision. The times are progressively leading us up to the big one.

I believe that God knows those who have the hidden attributes within themselves to accept His offer of sonship. Many are legitimately called, all have an equal opportunity to respond to the call, and those who ultimately come through with teachable, humble hearts will be the ones who are chosen. This is fair to everyone. No one can charge God with unfairness. It's up to us. In my case, a person would need an active imagination to believe that my old person could ever become moldable and pliable in God's hands. One might need this active imagination, but one also might not know the potential when the love of God is applied. This love did it for me, and this is what allowed me to change. God loves me. He really loves me!

God has two carrots: heaven and His love down here now. That love down here now was what I needed. Heaven was too far away; I needed help now.

22

Poverty, Work, and Eating

Our youngest son Chad called recently from Honduras where he, his wife, and over a hundred others from their church were on a mission trip there to build a first-time school in a rural area. They took two thousand pairs of shoes, food, and instructors to train untrained teachers. Chad's first day of work was with a pick and shovel. He told me that several young Honduran boys, seven years old or so, had volunteered to drive the wheelbarrow full of dirt for them. The boys worked all day with no breaks. One boy in particular had gotten Chad's attention because he owned no shoes. While telling me about this barefoot boy who would not stop working, I interrupted Chad and said, "Can we get him some shoes and maybe some other things?" Chad's answer was, "We're getting them now."

Earlier, I mentioned Mike Clark's school and orphanage in Guatemala, which I had visited on a similar mission trip. The native people there work from about 7:00 AM to 8:00 PM in the hot sun, using shovels and picks to build schools. No concrete mixers were used. The purpose for stating this is to frame the subject for this chapter: "Poverty, Work, and Eating."

We in America have taken the wrong approach to those who are needy. Our approach is making cripples of people who should be able-bodied producers. In no way do I take lightly the need to care for those who can't care for themselves, but we don't use this formula to determine need; we just give out what is now called benefits.

I'm no social activist, but I can back up these words with past actions. I have gone into prisons. I also have spent all of my teacher retirement money on a school for inner-city kids, mostly black kids in Gadsden, Alabama. I started the school from scratch with the help of a great role model, Dr. Bernard Gant of Cornerstone School in Birmingham. My school was the single most exciting project of my life, but it ended in failure after only eight months. That's another story for another day, but the bottom line is that I tried—I paid a heavy price—but I did something with my own hands.

We do not have real poverty in America today, at least not the kind of poverty as in much of the world. Many of the people that we call poor eat very well—you can tell this by just looking at them. The same people must have much time to eat, because you see them out in droves during the day at Wal-Mart and such. Many of these people also partake in the dog tracks and casinos. The Bible says that those who don't work shouldn't eat. That's a far cry from what we practice here today.

We even feed inmates in our prisons well, at least at the ones that I've attended. Work there is optional. Many inmates choose to work out with weights, play basketball, or watch those sexy soap operas. We have things all wrong.

I recommend that all Christians take a mission trip to Honduras or Guatemala. These countries have open-air garbage dumps at which hundreds of children get all of the day's food. At Mike Clark's orphanage, the police bring the kids to him from these dumps. The children are then named for the policemen who brought them. There are no records or anything, just the kids. Mike's orphanage has a baby dorm, which accommodates about one hundred babies up to about three years of age. When we went into the baby dorm, we sat in their rocking chairs and were immediately covered with babies to be rocked. In America, we've got it wrong!

A late update to the story about Chad's Honduras trip: If you remember, there were two seven-year-old boys who worked very hard without any shoes. I asked Chad if we could take care of the shoes, and he said that they were already working on it. Now, here's the rest of Chad's story. There were two boys from one family who worked, and there was an older brother who didn't work. Chad and his friend from Brookhills went out and bought all three boys two pairs of shoes each. Upon receiving his shoes, the older child broke down in tears.

Here's the part that I'm most proud to tell. The school that the workers were building was located on a very steep, long mountain road. Each day the workers needed to take all of their equipment and some supplies up that road by hand. Chad told me that on their last day, as they trekked up the long road, the two companion workers were talking about how much harder the task of moving the equipment had become over the one-week period, as fatigue had come upon them. As they were saying this and thinking how hard the work had become, they heard the three boys yelling to them from up top. The boys waited for them every day from an early hour. Upon hearing the boys yell, Chad said to his friend, "This task has now become much easier. God has blessed me with three wonderful boys."

Lest anyone get the opinion that I am too hard and that I speak out of both sides of my mouth, let me explain my views on this *no work, no eat* issue. To start, remember the chapter called "Bubba." I most definitely was a Bubba and still am a Bubba in this world today. I know the hurt of being rejected, and I know how to do without. When I was about ten or eleven years of age, the city of Gadsden had a big Christmas parade. In those days, it was safe for children to go out on their own within reason. Prior to the actual parade, I was in the big Sears, Roebuck and Company store looking at the toys for my own short Santa list. Standing beside me were a younger black boy and his dad. The little boy asked his dad if Santa could bring him a certain toy that year. The dad's reply was, "Son, I don't think you will be able to get that this year." This touched me down deeply. I'll never forget it.

I definitely have a heart for the poor of whatever color or nationality. In fact, I have probably too much of a heart for them. I just can't watch the things on TV that show the hurt of people. My feeling about the system today is that we're creating more hurt than we're curing. Giving something to someone over an extended period of time can damage the soul. It is similar in ways to Pavlov's Dog experiment. People can be trained to be dependent on the stimulus. Over time, this can be turned into anger and even rage. People are created to achieve. When achievement is lacking, all sorts of "stinkin thinking" emerges.

23

Racism and Civil Rights

This chapter, while not being located in the last position, may well be the last one written for this book. As you may have detected, this book is a work in progress. This chapter on racism could be the last because I can't think of a more provocative or controversial topic. Racism is a topic in which I do have some experience and even some expertise.

I've spoken before about my experiences in the early days of the civil rights movement. Here now is a brief review of some other experiences. At both of my first two coaching jobs as an assistant coach, we trail blazed the first black football players: Jesse Roberts at Choctawhatchie, and Willie Kirkland at Dothan. Each of these firsts was handled properly and was accomplished with no problems.

Problems, however, did arise at my next school, Hale County High in Moundville, which was located in what is called the Black Belt of Alabama. The label "Black Belt" is due to the color of the soil, I suppose, but also because the black population outnumbers the whites there greatly. This town was also my father's birthplace.

The problem arose in the spring of my first year there when my principal, Leo Sumner, told me of a black kid named Curtis Gray, who then attended the all-black school in town. Leo had only seen this boy play basketball because that school did not play football. Leo and I got into his old yellow pickup and began to recruit this kid for our predominantly white school where I coached. Curtis would be the first black football player in the county in 1969.

Curtis showed up from his school to practice with us one day and was issued equipment for our spring training. From the beginning, without knowing even how to put on his equipment, Curtis Gray would become almost a legend. He would acquire the nickname from the press of "The Gray Ghost." Curtis scored a touchdown the very first time he touched a football in practice. He had professional ability and was even recruited by Coach Bryant, but due to poor grades he was sent to Oklahoma to a junior college to become eligible.

We took Curtis on the bus with the team to our spring jamboree game, but he did not dress up that night. The following week at our regular countywide teacher's meeting,the superintendent of education notified us that all principals and coaches would meet with him that day. In the meeting, we were told with no room for uncertainty that we were not to recruit players from the black schools. Leo and I were hard of hearing on this however and never slowed down on bringing Curtis over to be a Wildcat.

The Gray Ghost was a great kid as were Jesse Roberts and Willie Kirkland. I never saw any mistreatment of Curtis until we went to a certain town to play. We were running up huge scores behind Curtis, and on this particular night we were ahead 28–0 late in the second quarter. The referees for this game were led by a man who had ties to the all-white private schools. Late whistles from these officials were allowing the opponents to stand Curtis up while attempting to tackle him. Upon being stood up, the other players were allowed to hit him late, which brought me onto the field several times for conferences with the officials. As a result of the officials sending me off the field and my subsequent telling them where they should go, the game was abruptly called. Before I even got to my sideline, I heard the opponents' band playing and their fans cheering. That game was over for the night.

A Sunday afternoon meeting was called with each school s coaches and principals, the game referee, and state athletic department officials. Within a couple of days, we were notified that I, along with the head referee, was being placed on one-year probation. The score of the game was settled: Hale County 28, Opponents 0.

I also came into direct contact with the black community as I participated in the Kairos Prison Ministry at St. Clair Correctional. My closest friends there were black inmates.

My most active and most enlightening experience came next. Upon retiring from the public schools, I felt a call to open a school in Gadsden, Alabama, along the lines of a very successful inner-city school, Cornerstone School in Birmingham. The work being done there was exciting in its potential for positive changes for disadvantaged kids. My school, Turning Point School, joined a national association, called the Hoboken Group of Schools, with similar goals. Two men became my close friends, Dr. Bernard Gont, a black educator who is now in Colorado Springs with a national association, and Moulton Williams, a prosperous white insurance man who devoted much time and money to Cornerstone.

I attended a national meeting of the Hoboken Group in Birmingham that allowed my vision to be enhanced. At a closing session the last night of the conference, the topic for a roundtable discussion was racism. Four speakers, all black, gave short speeches, and discussion was to follow. All four speakers spoke in basically the same vain—*poor old me, poor old us, how we are treated.* These speakers were all college-educated, well-dressed, private-school directors from around the country.

After hearing these talks I was the first to raise my hand to speak. I said, "You are black; however, you probably have twenty-twenty vision. I am white and am almost legally blind. You see life now through your black skin. I saw life for about fifty years through my thick glasses and the right eye that drifted to the side. When I was in school I could not read the material on the blackboard so I was forced to walk up to the board. This was looked upon by me with great shame and dread." This was my blackness.

When I came to Jesus Christ I may have brought this shame with me for a few years. I then learned, however, that God knew me from the beginning. He knew about my vision problem. He did not heal me of this problem. As I learned to love God, I gradually learned to accept myself just as I was, poor vision and all.

The nut of what I desire to say on racism is this: Feeling sorry for one's self and acquiring a bad attitude is not walking with God. I'm not addressing the black nonbelievers now; I'm addressing those who call themselves believers. You may have been called to a much higher calling than you ever imagined. You have been called to show examples of unity, unity with whites, tans, and blacks. To do this you have no room for all of that looking back and feeling sorry for yourself. You may have been up at the blackboard until now with shame. If need be now, you must go up there to the blackboard and smile with the right attitude. This is what I call *taking a hit*. You have been blessed. You should serve as an example to all those who are now mad and breaking their coke bottles upon the curb.

If we look back with honesty over the past fifty years, there has been a heck of a lot of positive things that have occurred. If those who are breaking the coke bottles and poking their lips out with the attitude of anger would just take a look back over the fifty years, they might appreciate things more now. They might also look over to Africa, or even Guatemala, to improve some "stinkin thinking," as my old motivator Zig Zeigler would say.

I promise this to be true: If you will be open to unity and love with all your brothers—black, white, and tan—you will receive love in return. To be open, you may need to be prepared to take the first step, and then the second step, but you will find unity out there. Don't do it the easy way, *do it the right way,* and your class will tell.

24

Proving God

Now I've come to the big moment, the time to put up or shut up. Earlier in the introduction I stated that I would attempt to prove the very existence of God. I'm not backing down on this, so here it goes. Let me explain something: I think that God may be allowing me to jump into this because of the stupid statements that I once made while socializing with some friends in their pool house over a few drinks. I made the statement, which was even more foolish than the ones they were making, that you shouldn't count too much on the existence of God.

I'm beginning this by saying unequivocally that God can be proven and I can do it. I'm not going to do it with some lightweight, mamby-pamby, religious jargon. I'm proving this by the miracles, which I have experienced both personally and as being witness to the lives of others. These miracles cannot be explained in any other way except as the hand of God being applied directly to the lives of those involved.

The first miracle that I will offer is the life of James E. Glover, or Coach Glover. My father was drawn to repent from his old life and to believe in Jesus the first Monday following his last football victory over Gadsden High, his biggest rival. My father soon received power to share Christ with his friends and ex-players. He became new in his life at home and to his boys. These were profound changes, but there were others also. My dad soon took up selling and delivering azaleas for his brother in Mobile. He made quite a lot of money doing this. This money was used at age sixty-two to start a much needed savings account. Then, as my company Promar was started through his insistence that we purchase the rights to do a Bear Bryant commemorative candle, he became my first and best salesman. He led our entire sales force until he retired from this to coach again at Coosa Christian School. At age seventy, my father began coaching again at Coosa Christian School. This new beginning ended with a national Christian school championship. He defeated a team from Washington, D.C., for the championship.

You may say that I haven't given enough proof yet of the existence of God. You're right. Let's move now into my own life. For the previous ten years before my turn in the coffee shop, I had literally never gone to bed without enough hard liquor to knock me out from the pain of the day. When I returned home from the hospital on the day of the coffee shop incident, I sat with Karen at our pool house explaining what had occurred the previous night. I remember having a drink, one only, that night.

Later, maybe two weeks or so, I was at the hospital in Birmingham where I explained to an ex-football player from Etowah how God had healed my alcoholism. Argus Kelley, who must have experienced the same problem with alcohol, then told me that I should not take even one drink. I took his advice, and I went cold turkey. God had healed me.

The healing for me was a real healing. I did not get new strength. I was healed. People attend the twelve-step programs today, and I've taught at some of these, but God's best is healing, not steps. Steps are the second best method to correct a serious, serious problem.

Now, can anyone explain to me any possible way that the total abstinence from alcohol could occur as easily as this occurred without a divine intervention from God? Can anyone give an explanation also of how a person who had plunged into such deep depression over the mere thoughts of losing his business could actually move through this very event calmly? The reality of the actual events that occurred during the closing of Promar was far worse than I ever imagined; yet I looked them in the eye as they occurred.

I can remember one incident that caused a crucial point of decision. Our company was selling a candle product that was being imported from Asia. The oil in the wax was defective and had caused five separate small fires within the first week after distribution. I was faced with the possibility of our candles, which may have been purchased by students as gifts for their parents, causing deaths. I could see those candles being lit around wrapping paper at Christmas. By making the decision to recall forty thousand candles, a line in the sand was drawn between Promar and a very powerful Chicago importer. This importer later took a big step towards shutting us down.

I could go on and on about the personal evidence, but let's move now into the lives of my family members. Prior to the demise of my business, my wife Karen, while very skillful, was only a hard worker. You should see what she does now and what has been done through her. I'm not going to delve into this any deeper because it might not please her to do so, but God's hand has obviously been applied to her career.

Again, I don't want to intrude into their privacy here, but our boys have been wonderfully gifted and blessed by God also. One son in particular is sort of our miracle son; he's that because he's needed miracles. He also seems to have the childlike faith needed to receive miracles. While in high school he was driving his Toyota when it flipped six times end over end. The two girls who were sitting in the front seat with him were ejected through a small hatchback window in the rear. There's too much here to go fully into, but God moved into this situation by sending angels to gently guide the girls to the ground. There were injuries that have been totally healed, but without prayer and God's hand this could have been really bad.

Then there was the time this same son was telling me on the phone that he had experienced some financial problem that had him concerned. I was traveling along an interstate in southern Mississippi at the time and suggested to him that we pray for help. I want to point out here that in this instance, as well as the instance of the car wreck, prayers went up to God through Jesus, not for God's will to be done, *but for His help*. God heard the prayers both times. Within no more than twenty minutes he called me on my cell phone, telling me that upon walking into his office he was given a ten-thousand-dollar bonus immediately, and five thousand dollars was to come soon. It's just too late to tell me that God isn't real. I actually haven't done justice to fully explaining the miracles surrounding his life, there have been so many. He is the current president elect of The Young Lawyers of America, how's that for a kid who grew up on Ritalin?

I've saved the biggest miracle and proof for last. This miracle and proof of God's existence is back to my life again—the guy who wore those thick glasses, with the crooked teeth, that told fibs hoping to make people accept and respect him; the guy who painted the picture through his dreams, actions, and words that he really was worth being looked upon. That guy now knows who he is. He knows full well all the deception, all the foolish acts, and all the sordid deeds that he has committed. He also now knows that the real person, the one he is becoming today, was seen by God all along. It just took some time to develop.

For this day in time, these are the types of miracles that God performs most often. After all, it is the actual life that He truly desires. It's the life, not our service, works, or sacrifice.

I've seen much more that could be shared as actual miracles, but I say also that I've seen many that could be questionable as to the source. The devil cannot counterfeit one miracle however the changed life. I was never allowed to wear one of those crimson blazers at Alabama, but I wear a new robe now, the robe of righteousness, and I am preparing now for the day when my robe will be white by the blood of the Lamb (Revelation 7:14).

25

I Am Who I Am

When Moses was told to go to Pharaoh and give him God's message to let His people go, Moses asked Him, "Who shall I say sent me? Or in what name do I say this?" God's reply was to tell Pharaoh that "I Am Who I Am sent me."

I've sought in my life the thing that is *real,* the real deal. This search meant following various leaders at times and various ideologies. The very first leader was my father, whose style left much to be desired in the areas of tenderness and mercy, and who was powerful in his authoritarianism. At college, Coach Bryant used authoritarian techniques also.

Robert Schuler of the Crystal Cathedral and the Hour of Power, with his concept of positive thinking, along with motivator Zig Zeigler, gave me leadership later. But I must admit that these methods and attempts at direction were effective only for a short time. All of this left me empty. My attempt at personally knocking down opposition or obstacles had failed utterly.

Down in the coffee shop in Gadsden that night in my time of despair, I spoke out to God and in effect asked, *If you are who you seem to be in my father's life, will you be that to me?* His reply was, *I am who you hope that I am,* and instantly He proved who He was to me.

How can I make the point with pen and ink those things which I know in my heart to be true? Jehovah, God—the creator of the universe, the Father of Jesus Christ—has set the absolute basis for all reality. His reality is actually the entirety of all that we see and feel with our eyes and hands. He has created all that there ever will be. His reality is the only true reality. Our mere reality in actuality is only that which we are able to understand, see, and receive. The reality for one person is not that for another.

The biggest and most important questions in all of life are: Who controls our reality? How close to the real reality are we able to come? The truly wise people will see, and thereby attain, the benefits of their understood truth. Others, operating in delusion or less understanding, will capture only the benefits that their faulty understanding will provide.

God is real. He is who He says He is. This is the ultimate reality. Those who are operating outside His kingdom can only see with their limited old understanding mere shadows of His wonderful works. His concept of telling deep truths by the means of parables is a good example of this. Full understanding comes only to those who, as I say, *jump off the cliff into life with Jesus*—no looking back, no changing our minds.

We all start off with only the faith given to us by God, but our ability to utilize this faith grows as we grow by the prescribed method, feeding upon His word. We feed ourselves on that which is nutritional. I believe wholeheartedly the following statements (there are absolutely no shortcuts to this): We must start off with the correct means, true repentance, and real faith, and we continue by feeding on Jesus' words. He is real food, his flesh is real food, and his blood is real drink for life. With His huge investment in Jesus for us, there is no allowance for our stubbornness and individuality. Coach Bryant told us two or three times each year, "You must not do it the easy way; *do it the right way.*" The right way is God's way, and we who are His know who He is. He is "I Am," He is who He says that He is, and He backs it up.

26

Why Are There Still Monkeys?

In 2005 Jeremiah Castille, the great University of Alabama defensive back who is now a minister with the Fellowship of Christian Athletes, spoke in Albertville at a men's conference. He made a humorous statement about the untruthfulness of evolution. The statement was, "If evolution is true and we did evolve from monkeys, then why are there still monkeys today?" This humorous story brings focus to important issues: personality defects, quirks, and soulish ties. Some soulish ties are perfectionism, control Spirit, and such. These are not to be confused with addictions and habits that are known, but not under control. These soulish ties are repressed in our psyche and hidden.

Now, let's get to the proper message that God wants to be given—I think that I have it now. Why can I write this book now after struggling for twenty years to know my calling? There were monkeys out there that would have belied the message that I would have been speaking. Was I hardheaded, or were the monkeys in so deeply that it just took a long time for them to come out fully enough? I don't know which of these was true—or both—but it did take much time, and honestly the biggest release has come very recently.

Was I born again twenty years ago? Did I love God? Yes, I certainly did. Could I speak truth in any useful way? Probably not. I think that I was *locked down* with delusion within my personality for many years even after my rebirth. I was *locked down* for six or seven years to thoughts of pornography—not any actions, just thoughts. I was *locked down* to an inferiority complex for ten years or so. I was abruptly alerted to my Spirit of control after about ten years. The bottom line is that even after rebirth I was still messed up. I could go to prisons and speak big things, but inside I was still messed up.

Now, the previous message was not an attempt at self-confession for the purpose of my own cleansing; it was for those others out there who also have monkeys. Monkeys are out there today. I know they are because I see them living in people who love God. Can a person with monkeys make it to heaven? Probably, but do we really want to put Christ back upon the cross? At our baptism we committed ourselves to die with Christ. This death is intended to include all areas of our old nature. 2 Corinthians 5:17 states, "We are a new creation, old things are passed away, behold all things have become new."

You've read too much of my writings by now to not know that this becoming new to me means progressively becoming new, not instantly becoming new. The proof that we belong to Christ is that the Holy Spirit lives in us, and He does the work to teach and cleanse us. We must let Him work.

Could anyone have confronted me early in my walk with Christ with the things that were mentioned earlier? Yes, they could have confronted me, but I would have rejected the knowledge. At that time I had not completed testing my love for God. It really is *only your love for God* that will enable you to be open to your quirks and to forcibly remove them. When this love is developed properly *we just can't now bear the thoughts of Christ being defamed* by our lives.

27

Persecution

Regardless of what we say that seems holy and religious, no person in his right mind really likes to be abused or persecuted. Most of us want things to flow smoothly. Smoothly, however, has not been the way one would describe my life of twenty years with Jesus. My prosperity has come in the area of my soul, but not my bank account. For the ten years prior to my coming to Christ, I had been a very ugly abuser of money, so maybe I needed some dryness to correct this.

The apostle Paul states that all who desire to live Godly will suffer persecution, not just hard times, but persecution. This persecution comes at the hands of two sources: the devil and man. Actually, I believe that while God wants all good things for us, he knows that without our letting go of the bad things, the selfish things, and the old soulish things, we will never become holy. So, He allows the devil to shake them away from us if we just let go. If we won't let go, Satan wins. God did say that we would be holy because He is holy. While God knows all things about us, the devil knows of the weak things in us also. We know that the devil is the accuser of the brethren and likes to show off our shortcomings to God.

I think that God probably allowed Satan to take away my business. Keeping it would have distracted and tempted me. He attacked it with great power, undeniably supernatural power. Also, many other things that would later need to be removed from my life would be removed. Much of this later removal was a result of the bad seed that I had personally planted. Bad seed as well as good seed must grow to be a crop.

I tenaciously held to some soulish things that God also needed to remove, the biggest of which was a Spirit of control. This Spirit of control had been developed early in life; it could be seen in my pouting, my trickery, and my plotting. In later years, this Spirit developed into more over-powering manifestations designed to get my way. I was forced to admit these truths one day when I was telling some very spiritually mature friends about someone else who operated this same control Spirit. To my surprise, they called me later that day and agreed with me about the other person, but also said, "You have it, too." I confessed and repented immediately and took steps to keep this in order.

I am not the only one who had or now has this Spirit of control; it is very big today. It is seen on pulpits, on TV, in commercials, and especially in homes. The role model that we are to follow personally is God. Then, we are to leave other people on their own. Of course, children are about the only exception. I've seen some pretty extreme examples of people who are powerfully into this Spirit of control. This Spirit is an extremely difficult one with which to reason or compromise. This Spirit wants to dominate. It uses deception, manipulation, pouting, and even temper tantrums to establish and maintain control.

Back now to the forms of persecution. The number one persecutor is the very real devil; he enjoys it. The number two persecutors believe it or not, are religious people, not to be confused with real Christians. Maybe this shouldn't surprise us since it was those same people who crucified our Lord. The actual thing that gets them going most often is the realization that you may feel, or show that you may be, different, especially with regard to the Holy Spirit. This was the thing that caused Jesus trouble also.

The task of sorting out the tares from among the wheat is reserved for God. I've wanted to help out in the past, but have been educated on the matter now. By the words of Jesus when explaining His only two commands of the new covenant, we are to love God with all of our heart, mind, and strength. This grabbed my attention when I first saw it. How much does God expect? What kind of obedience and fellowship does He expect? It's pretty clear to me. He expects it all. The second commandment is the real test here on Earth. No one knows how much we love God, but God. But it's pretty obvious that we don't love the brothers in Jesus down here properly. God expects us to be tolerant of those with different views on minor issues. The blood shed at Calvary for my sins is not one of the minor issues. This blood was shed for anyone who would accept it as the atonement for their sins and those who would make a genuine commitment to live a new life in His sacrifice.

28

Hardness of Heart

There is a condition that has been discussed here over and over by utilizing differing phrases and examples—examples such as the robo plastic man, the goody-two-shoes type, the self-centered type, the falsely sophisticated type, and the religious type who has fixed himself upon the incorrect object. These may all be classified as one general condition—a hardened heart against the true standard, that standard of the heart of real faith in God.

We see ample evidence today of man's hardened condition in the ugly, evil, and atrocious criminal acts of seemingly heartless people. These acts are certainly deplorable and seem to be increasing. This, however, is not the only area of concern; the average citizen's general hardness of heart is apparent also. Sure, we may give money freely to victims of disasters, and this is good, but what about the little things, such as hurtful language, rumors, and gossip in which we heartlessly participate? We're becoming hardened by necessity today for our protection's sake against the general onslaught of harsh words. Also, what about the constant strain placed upon us today to protect ourselves from being ripped off or victimized by corruption? This forces more hardness upon us.

We are being forced to become harder, more alert, and more savvy for the reasons mentioned before. Also, just as a constant rubbing against the heel of your foot will cause a callous, this environment will cause our hearts to form a callous. The most serious hardness of heart condition, and one that I think has a direct tie to those mentioned here, is the condition mentioned by Jesus in Mark 6:52. Jesus was admonishing his disciples for their hardness of heart. He stated that their "hearts were hardened." The disciples had just experienced His feeding of the five thousand, but were taken in fright by boisterous winds as they rowed by night upon the sea. It was not that they were callous to life, or to Jesus, or that they were insensitive to people—they just didn't see with spiritual eyes. This was the hardness of heart.

Matthew chapter 13 contains the most important teaching in parable form by Jesus. It is the parable of the seed. Beginning at verse 12, we learn that whosoever has spiritual ears shall be given more understanding, and those who do not have spiritual ears will lose even the things they think they have learned. Verse 13 states, "They shall in seeing, see not, in hearing hear not, neither shall they understand."

The principal fact to remember here is that the condition of the heart is vital. In verse 15, Jesus states that the majority of people's hearts in that teaching were waxed gross, their ears were dull of hearing, etc. Lest at any time they may see with their eyes, or hear with their ears and should understand and be converted and God may be able to heal them Mathew 13: 15..

The above teaching is so important; it is our heart condition that determines our destiny. It sure appears that hardness of heart has taken on epidemic proportions today, but one thing is true also about this. While many hearts are waxed gross until the end, God's workings can resurrect some of the very hardest ones back to life.

The worst condition that a human can have is a condition called *stone deafness to God's voice.* Just as those who are totally deaf to even the loudest noises have no hope, those who are stone deaf to God's voice have no hope as well. This is a condition in which one has used up his last chance.

Spiritual understanding is absolutely necessary in the walk with Jesus. It first begins when we discover our spiritual ears, and then it grows as we absorb the good seed of the word of God.

29

A Definition of Grace

Every church person knows the Scripture in Ephesians 2:8 that states that we are saved by grace through faith. In Galatians 2:21, Paul asks the Galatians not to frustrate the grace of God by going back from the life of faith to our old ways. I think that I may have already made a big point on this but I will proceed further.

Faith, the real kind, activates a relationship with God called grace. In common terms this allows us to be considered holy and blameless in times during which we are not truly holy and blameless. God's program requires that we do not *frustrate* this grace during our time here. Actually, this time lasts the remainder of our lives; it is not finished until we are fully redeemed in heaven. The frustrating of God's grace seems to be the time when we show signs of slowing this growth in holiness and even stopping it. By stopping this growth, we put the Lord back upon the cross by our saying in essence, *I've sacrificed enough now.*

You may read examples of my own current boldness and my mighty stances on God that I now take. Let me now give an actual everyday example of grace. I was bold in my stances eighteen years ago. This is the working example of grace: Eighteen years ago, or even ten years ago, my claims were not based upon reality in the truest sense. I was operating in a state of grace and am still doing so today. I received a favor from God because my actual performance was shy of the standard, which is holiness. Eighteen years ago the integrity or character of my testimony would have been suspect. I'm not completely innocent today, but I've come a great distance from where I was at that time. This is grace, God giving us time to live up to the standard.

Some churches place most of the emphasis of grace at the point where we first enter into the kingdom by faith. I think that my old friends in Methodism and the Walk to Emmaus have it more accurately. They teach two types of grace: that which is called *saving grace,* and the continuing grace called *sanctifying grace.* One grace alone is incomplete.

The all-inclusive identification of all of those people who call themselves Christians sure gives the outside world a poor image today of Christianity. Wolf, Jack, and their New Age counterparts paint Christianity with too wide a brush, however. Not all who call themselves Christians are really known by God.

Our new coach here at Alabama made a couple of very significant statements following our recent losses and near losses. The first statement was, "No team on our schedule will roll over just because we're Alabama." The second was, "Image is how you look in your uniform; real integrity is how you play." Here in Alabama those fans of the University of Alabama have been living for over a quarter century in the past integrity and image. Integrity looks good during the game out on the field. This sounds much like Coach Wyman Townsel's look-good loser analogy.

Our real uniform as Christians is when we are stripped naked, placed upon a cross, cut, and whipped. Standing on the sideline wearing a neat and clean uniform does not enable us to be called real players. Real players move into sanctification and holiness. Our uniforms get soiled during this process.

30

The Changed Life

I know what a changed life for Jesus looks like. Now, let's see if I can describe it. This topic came about after our forty-fifth high school reunion. All of us are now over sixty years of age and have mellowed very much. One thing that struck me was that my classmates have gotten very vocal about the mighty works of Jesus. We had a time of sharing, where each class member told of the big events in his life. God has done some mighty works there, and my classmates were quick to give Him honor and praise.

The biggest attention-getter for me was Gilbert Morton, who was one co-captain—along with myself and Jimmy Kell—of the 1961 Blue Devils. Gilbert has made what I would call an amazing turnaround and is an extremely vocal advocate of Jesus Christ. Gilbert is now blind and relies upon someone to lead him everywhere. I know a change when I see one; Gilbert is an example of one.

This may be just my own observation and not factual, but from my vantage point those who change drastically are usually those who needed much change, myself included. It appears that for this observable change to occur in a way that is detectable, the changing person must have observable character needs. The Bible points this out also when it states that not many noble people are called. Rather, the base things are called so that God, not man, can receive the glory.

Youth ministries are great, but their actual value must lead them to the same end as the Gilbert Mortons, Jerry Glovers, and Jim Glovers. Actually all ministry should have the same end.

I assembled a small tri-fold brochure recently titled "Too Messed Up To Be Nice." In this brochure I explained how, for me and I think many others, it was impossible to make the transition from being really messed up all the way to being considered nice, ordinary Christians. The chief reason for this is probably that we're just so excited about this change. We're also very messed up.

I doubt that Billy Graham, Mike Clark (the missionary to Guatemala whom I've mentioned), and many other seasoned Christian leaders ever reacted in the manner of those who are mentioned above. However, it does appear that some other leaders of our heritage have done so. John Wesley, who is my foremost hero, must have had a supercharger working in him as he preached in pastures at five o'clock in the morning.

I think that there is one thing that cannot be held within a truly changed person. That one thing is: *I know that God lives in me, I know that I'm changed, something has happened in me.* My father lived for only eight or nine years after receiving Christ into his heart. He was noisy the entire time. As of June 2, 2007, I have lived for twenty years as a believer. I'm quieter now than I was ten years ago, but now I'm wiser in choosing my shots.

In these twenty years I have seen some amazing things happen in the lives around me. I've also been unwise at times, giving people undeserved credit for their beliefs. Following is a story that proves that I had actually been correct in my early opinion of an inmate who for a time looked very much like a hypocrite.

I'm not using his name here, but when I first became involved in the Kairos Prison Ministry I was fascinated by the powerful use of God's words from some of the inmates. I had especially been impressed by two black inmates who I increasingly became close to and involved with. One of the inmates had asked me once to help get him a non-court-appointed lawyer to appeal his lifetime conviction. I did this to no avail, and he remains in prison today.

Another favor that he asked of me ultimately revealed to me that he was operating in a homosexual relationship with another inmate who had been transferred to another prison. Now, I'm not judging that type of relationship here, but this lifestyle was not what he was portraying in his role as assistant to the chaplain. Upon receiving undisputable knowledge of this affair, I confronted him with this as I understood it was the proper thing to do as a Christian. He vehemently denied this and even fooled the ministry leaders about this when another brother and I took the matter to them. As a result of our taking this public, I was suspended from the prison for one year.

The bottom line to this story is that approximately three years after his being allowed to escape any repercussion from this accusation, he stood up in a service one night and publicly confessed. Upon confessing he went to my brother in the faith, Milford, and asked him to please tell Brother Glover about what happened here tonight. What happened really was that he had been real all along, with a huge stain that God would remove. Confessing this was a very dangerous thing for any inmate to do, much less a chaplain's helper.

Real-life changes show evidence of change. If there's no evidence that can be detected then, there's no way that I can identify and join with them—I won't know who they are. All people who have been changed are not noisy; some just quietly get to work for the kingdom of God. One thing that I do know for sure, however, is that it will be obvious that they're working for the kingdom of God, not some religious or social cause. Jesus Christ's name will come out. They will be name-droppers for sure.

31

Religiosity

I use a negative word here to represent my feelings on the topic of dead religion. Religiosity is the practice of attempting to worship the very real God in an unreal manner. This topic may provoke those people who wish to continue practicing this exercise in futility. For clarity's sake, I will give some guidelines here to identify this practice.

To fully discuss this topic we must set some parameters. There are two extremes to consider. Those extremes are: those who worship in a manner that omits God's true nature and those who go too far so as to presume this nature. Both extremes are false. If you'll just take my word on this, I've participated in both extremes and I know what I'm talking about on this subject.

The first group, those who worship through omission, are pretty easy to detect by their funeral home dryness. In fact, they seem to have a reverence for death. My wife Karen, upon leaving such a service, once was exasperated as she said, "Where do these preachers get that stuff? They must have books from which they get those sermons."

On another occasion, while dwelling upon that same type of sermon and that type of worship, I asked Karen how people could look at heaven, and especially at hell, and follow as they do these religious forms. Karen's response about the hell issue was, "They just don't think that it'll be that bad. Do I need to say more?"

Now to the other extreme: those who presume upon God's name and nature. May I say that I'm also an expert on this. I've participated as a very loose follower in some extremely ugly things, from which I have now fully turned. These overzealous, self-seeking believers have brought much false information and false image into the public's perception of true religion. Here are some common abuses today:

- the conjuring up of signs and wonders through the hands of man, not God

- the raising of money for the ministry through promises of reward for those who will have enough faith to give

- the promises of personal financial prosperity for those who will have faith to believe for it

- the placing of a man in between the believer and Jesus

- the use of show-business tactics to conduct worship

The detection of error in both cases is sometimes hard because those in leadership are very good at what they do. To detect the first group, the omission group, one can listen to the intensity level and the wording of their prayers. There is no anticipation of God's response, only hollow words. This group seems to be praying to a dead God.

The detection of the presumption group is also easy for the trained eye, for the one who has learned his way through direct experience with his error. These people go too far in their zeal and actually proposition God for His performance. But with the unreal, there is also the real. Here are some things to identify those who are real:

1. The glory for all of life's blessings goes to God only.

2. When these people pray they are careful about the selected topics from which to pray. One can detect an expectation of a positive response coming back from God when prayer goes forth.

3. They are not showy or vain in their appearance, their presentations, or their lifestyles.

I can hear people saying now, *Jerry, you're setting the bar too high. No one qualifies. Yes, they do,* is my unqualified answer. Not as many as some may think, but many do qualify.

The church that Karen and I now attend is perhaps the best large church that I've seen. I can say this because of the stances the pastors take. These pastors teach and believe that God can and will do something today. They also believe that He is doing something at places other than their own. They compete against sin and ignorance, not against other churches. The single biggest difference that I've noticed is that these guys can admit that they are not perfect. When I did this in my brief career as a preacher, my people nailed me.

Humility and faith are the elements that identify the real from the unreal. Humility, the real kind, cannot be faked. You either have humility or you don't. Faith is absolutely, unequivocally necessary. Hebrews 11:6 states, "Without faith it is impossible to please God." Most people today claim to have faith that God is real. Real faith speaks like this: Since God is real, I must respond appropriately to His realness.

32

What Balanced Believing Believes

Karen made this statement about nineteen years ago when I told her that I had a need and desire to preach, "Why, you'll start a new denomination." This has become prophetic to a degree. I do have a standard belief that I will discuss here. I know of only a few others who are preaching the exact same beliefs as I am. However, my denomination will never meet together in a building; it will only see my views in print. One does not need to totally accept every part of my position for me to receive him as a brother.

Here's what Balanced Believing doesn't believe:

1. A sole group has God's exclusive favor.

2. Being nice and doing good works are pleasing in their own right to God.

3. A onetime event can assure us of our salvation.

4. The presence of spiritual gifts signifies our acceptance by God.

5. A legalistic knowledge of God's word is a sign of our acceptance.

6. Speaking God's words aloud through memorization shows spiritual superiority.

Now that some of the most common things that Balanced Believing does not believe in have been revealed, what are the principles of Balanced Believing?

1. God does it all: He draws us, He gives us His faith, and He, through His Spirit, sees us through.

2. While He does it all, we do have a part. Our part is obedience. The true believer does have God's Spirit, but it is definitely possible to become stone deaf to that Spirit or to go to sleep (1 Corinthians 11:30).

3. Our part, the part of obedience, relies upon keeping our spiritual ears and eyes open and active. We must continually receive the good food of God's word. We cannot keep our conscience alert without active contact with the Holy Spirit.

4. Willful sin or rebellion will not be tolerated by God. The person who continues in this is headed back to his old life.

5. There is an enforcer who must be dealt with, the devil.

To summarize these points, I must say again that I do not presume to be a theologian or even a Bible scholar; I only know that which I have personally experienced and deduced. I have never found a plateau on which to land or a place to rest. With all of that said, even though I may have been an extreme example, I do not believe that anyone can find the path to be very different. My negatives may have been very obvious, but other people's negatives, while kept secret, could be just as corrupt.

Here's the journey that I feel we all must travel to become good soil:

1. We must have sincere repentance.

2. We must come to true faith in what God has done on Earth through Jesus.

3. We will be attacked by the devil in an attempt to scare us away from our faith.

4. Those soulish things that we are reluctant to give up must be dealt with and surrendered. The devil works to expose those things by accusing us before God. The devil then sets up a test that will either expose our defects or prove our faith.

5. As we walk with God by feeding upon His word, and as we've succeeded in foiling most of the plans of the enemy, our love for God grows. We then begin to be proven faithful. Our good soil brings forth a crop of good fruit.

6. The key to God's entire plan rests upon two tenets: Man must see our sin as it is, and then man must see Jesus dying on the cross for that sin. We will never make it through without those facts emblazoned upon our souls.

I've participated loosely in many organizations that promote a much less demanding approach to God. I haven't found that I could totally rely upon any of them. Some told me that rebirth was not required, and some told me that my actual rebirth was all that I needed. Some told me that the exercise of my spiritual gifts put me on a higher plane than those others.

The things that have worked for me, and the things that are my Balanced Believing platform, are that we must enter the kingdom by the prescribed manner. Once in the kingdom, we are to continue along the path of devotion and obedience to God. I personally believe that through proper teaching, many of the failures that I have experienced could have been eliminated and the time for growth could have been compressed. However, the big shortfall to this is: Where is the proper teaching? I think that with just the very basic truth about the devil's tactics, much of my loss could have been avoided. That's Balanced Believing: *Do it the right way.* Do not take shortcuts or the easy way. The stakes in this matter are too high.

33

The Watered-Down Gospel

In Galatians 1:9, Paul speaks of some men who were preaching another gospel rather than the one that he preached. He states that if any man preaches any other gospel than his, let that man be cursed. Let that false gospel be cursed and produce no fruit. What exactly is the gospel that Paul preached? 1 Corinthians 15:1–4 states this gospel very explicitly. The key elements of this are:

1. By *keeping in memory* those things that were preached by Paul and also *received* by us, we will be saved.

2. Christ *died* on the cross for the sins of man, according to the Scriptures.

3. Christ was buried and then *rose* again on the third day, according to the Scriptures.

The most misunderstood parts and those elements that have caused the most division are items 1 and 3. The issue of the supernatural aspect of the gospel is listed as number 3. Christ rose from the grave. Let there be no misunderstanding about this—this gospel is spooky, and there is nothing natural about it. This gospel cannot be made natural. Item 1 mentions how one successfully believes this spooky gospel, how someone keeps this gospel in his memory.

Here are the steps to be taken once one has determined that a change is needed in his life and a commitment to make that change has been consecrated. The person will then choose which gospel he will follow. There are many gospels as Paul has stated. If a person selects Paul's gospel, then a giant step of faith is required, which is the only way one can successfully receive this gospel. This step of faith could be described as similar to one's stepping off of a cliff. At the point of our first step we are not totally sure that we will land safely. We only have a hope based upon the reality that our old way must be changed and that this new way, Jesus, is what we will try. This word "try" is the key. Some people's try is limited by the low degree of their commitment. For those who succeed, their try is with all that they have; they do not leave back any means by which to return.

Those who step out with proper commitment will spend only a short time in suspense. God will catch them very quickly. Those who qualify their commitment will spend their entire life waiting for the catch or wondering if they were caught.

Most evangelical churches today tend to be of the more assertive variety. These churches do a good job of teaching the generalities of Paul's gospel. It's the specifics that need to be explained better. The specifics are the areas mentioned earlier, the supernatural nature and the effective method of believing the gospel. Many churches today, most I would even say, max out too early on the essentials and move on to the less controversial topics. Those less controversial topics usually are: self-improvement, devotion to the church, and financial prosperity.

Who would disagree that we in America today are self-centered and spoiled? We all feel deep down that we can have it our way. When we merely feel that pain is on the way, we can take measures to avoid it. In my life I've found that people almost always take a self-centered stance toward personal loss or sacrifice. Going through the loss of a company with 125 employees taught me this lesson very well.

Society today, in this democracy, is driven strongly by norms. Norms are what is *normal* or what *normal* people would like. These norms are directly related to numbers. Numbers are derived by the amount of an issue's appeal. Here's a simple example of how these norms affect life. First, we find out those things that are desirable, comfortable, and do not negatively affect our egos. Second, and finally, we go out and establish an entity to satisfy these desires. We can invent a product, start a new business, or maybe establish a new service to meet these desires. We can even apply the very same dynamics to the church. Today, we can make changes in areas that do not seem to be desirable or workable. This is exactly the message that Paul was expressing to the Galatians. Things that cannot be changed must not be changed.

Change has worked itself into the church mostly in the areas of lessening accountability and submitting to authority. This has become almost understandable since today there seems to be difficulty in determining that which is real. When one is uncertain, the wise thing to do may well be to stay aloof or noncommittal.

There is one other very significant reason for our changes in the church toward less authoritarian messages: People today get offended so easily. Offended people can find another place to attend. The pastor today may well feel that he has no ability to help a person who has departed, so he'll just do all that they will allow him to do. These and other factors do play roles in the watering down of the gospel today. While this watering down is certainly true, God is not deceived. Since there are no Pauls today, many of God's called and chosen are seemingly left alone as orphans, except for their own Bibles. God will have the last laugh. Those who are truly His will take their seed from His word, water it, tend it, and by caring for their own soil they become even stronger. Those who can get the good message on their own will never need a man to catch his fish for them. They can fish for themselves. This ability to fish for oneself does come to everyone who becomes good soil, but not quickly. Strong meat belongs to those who are full age (Hebrews 5:14).

34

Altar Calls, Baptism, and Counts

My ex-pastor, Mike Johnson, whom I dearly love and respect as a true Bible teacher, once made a statement during a service. He may not have meant the same conclusion that I received, but his statement was, "Up here on Sand Mountain it's hard to find someone who doesn't think that he is saved." Sand Mountain is a very religious area with over three hundred churches just in my old county alone. While very religious, it is also a good area with good people. I've learned to appreciate this even more since moving from there to Birmingham after thirty-three years. People in Marshall County are probably more naive and innocent than those in Jefferson County. You can get by just fine with those things there. It pays down here in Jefferson County to be cautious. You may get taken.

Back now to Mike's statement. The denomination in which I've spent the most years did not really use the word "saved." They talked about confirmations or conversions, but didn't use counts. Mike's denomination used the word "saved" for those who come down to the altar and make a public profession. They took counts of these. A third group, the Pentecostals, or Charismatics, also used the word "saved," but they put little emphasis on counts. Sometimes they mostly asked people to raise their hands as a sign of their salvation.

Regardless of where people worshipped in Marshall County, almost no one would admit to their not being saved. There were many who attended no church at all because of their excuse of church error or hypocrisy, but who also thought they were saved. These conditions may be prevalent in almost any area in the South.

Well, here's what I concluded from Mike's comment. If everyone is saved, is that which we see all that there is? These are outwardly nice, good people, but is this all there is to the real life in Jesus? The answer is no, this is not all. It is hard to experience the "all" everywhere since we're so leavened. There are at least three groups sitting in all services anywhere: the seekers, those who think they were found but never surrendered, and those who were found and surrendered.

A belief about the salvation of man that is accepted widely in the South is the "once saved, always saved" line of theology. This theology holds to the belief that one good trip to the altar and one good profession in Jesus is all that really is required for what is called "eternal security." Church attendance and a good life are proof to the authenticity of this profession.

Another facet of theology, Dispensationalism, is accepted very widely in the South also. The belief in Dispensationalism is that God does not deal with people directly today as He did with those in the Bible, especially the New Testament. This belief contends that we cannot expect God to perform miracles as He did then. My explanation is a gross exaggeration, but I think you'll get the point. I'm sure glad I didn't accept this doctrine the night my son Chris had that terrible accident. I believed that God would move his hands for those kids and He did.

When I first came to faith in Jesus Christ, I was still attending the denomination in which I was christened as a child. It was the same one where I had attempted to become a preacher. Today, I still retain much of the beliefs and also hold much love for those churches in both Attalla and Albertville. Soon, however, as in the case of my father who explained that he had switched churches so that he could see some people getting saved, I wanted to see this also. I dreamed to be able to attend a church that had those great altar calls and a church that sang "Just as I am, Without One Plea." Well, I've now been allowed to experience this with a mixed review of it.

I have now participated in ministries and witnessed many more that conducted this type of ministry. I've seen thousands of people make responses for Christ. I was working with a youth minister once who was conducting a session of Fellowship of Christian Athletes where 150 of about 175 athletes responded to the altar call. I've also participated in chemical dependency recovery ministries, which produced large numbers of responders.

Here are my feelings now after being involved and studying these things for twenty years. My father went to his knees on the Monday following his last public school football game on Friday. I started my walk with Jesus on June 2, 1987, in a coffee shop. Some people obviously respond to God's calling at a church service while others respond directly to God at another time and place. One key reason for our lack of unity and power in today's church is simply this; many so called believers are not clothed properly with their wedding garment, Jesus. We've pleaded for people to just, come on down; once they've come down we can then clean them up. That arrangement puts the cart ahead of the proverbial horse,it doesn't allow God to work. God doesn't work after the fact; He works to achieve the proper beginning, true repentance. By doing this man's hands become an obstacle to God. The proper approach is to be less assertive and more patient.

The vital factor is that they respond to God's calling, not to man's calling. It's really not very important how many numbers are counted; it is vitally important that we are counted as real by God. God can definitely receive us when His word is taught and preached by those whom He has appointed. In reality, this time at an altar, however, may just be the culminating point of what may have taken their entire lifetime to conclude. It can happen in an office or a coffee shop just as easily. A very well-known cynical, old lawyer over in western Alabama received the Lord while he was on the cardiac care table where he was undergoing a serious heart attack. He emerged powerfully and continuously as a witness for Jesus and is a sweet, sweet person. That friend of his and mine, who attended West Point and who is also a lawyer, is a sweet, sweet man also. There are many of us who are not wimps. I'm not alone. These guys are just as bold as me.

35

Rocky Balboa—Hope

Who hasn't walked out of a theater after watching a Rocky Balboa movie not feeling that he himself could conquer almost anything? I know that I have done this on many occasions. I've seen similar movies, such as *Rudy*, about the walk-on football player who persevered to play only in the final minutes of his final game at Notre Dame. I recently saw a movie called *Invincible* about a similar, off-the-street guy who made the team with the Philadelphia Eagles. These movies are mostly all fictional but portray an important picture, the picture of hope.

It is hope that gives life to me; it keeps me going. I can recall how in early years such as those in high school, college, and even early manhood, I would wake up with excitement thinking that something good was going to happen on that very day. As I grew into my middle years I woke up with just the opposite feeling; I hoped that nothing bad would happen on that day. It is hope that keeps us moving forward. In our mature years, our hopes are not the same as those of children hoping for Christmas Day to arrive. Mature hopes must be placed in something in front of us that has some substance to it.

I leave the Rocky Balboa movies wondering what will ultimately be Rocky's fate. I've seen examples, even in my own life, where people like Rocky may have had some great moments, but those moments were tempered by reality. Reality is that time moves on, and the things that were inside Rocky that made him into sort of a bum have not really changed. This reality is not one that usually has a happy ending. Even in the very best scenarios time will tarnish the glitter of life, and an end will someday arrive. We will all someday come to the end of life here as it has been.

1 Corinthians 15:12–19 states that if Christ had not risen from the dead then there is no resurrection. Any preaching on that subject would be false preaching, and those who believed in such a resurrection were of all men to be the most pitied.

According to Hebrews 11:1–3, faith is the substance of things hoped for, the evidence of things not seen. This goes on to tell that through faith we understand that the worlds were framed by the word of God so that things that are seen were not made by things that appear. This Scripture from the Bible tells us that there is hope that can be based upon something that is real but cannot be seen. The previous Scripture from 1 Corinthians tells us that there is hope for life, that the resurrection of Christ was real. This stuff is spooky. It is asking that we, instead of fixing our hopes on things that we can see down here, must place our hopes on the resurrection of Jesus Christ and this promise for eternal life with Him and God.

These teachings are extremely challenging. Do I fix my hopes on the resurrection as being real, or do I fix my hopes on my financial holdings, etc.? There is even a position in which many people attempt to hedge their bet by playing both numbers. Hedges don't work in this because the faith that is mentioned is real faith, not hedging faith. We must place our money upon only one number.

In Mark 10:21 Jesus tells the rich, young ruler to go sell all that he has because all of his other righteous deeds were insufficient for his eternal life. The rich, young ruler went away sorrowful because he had much riches and money. It's clear to me that Jesus is speaking here about choosing which path to take to insure eternal life. It doesn't seem that there is more than one option allowed. Sell all that you have, or keep going on as you were doing. Jesus is not telling us to go out and sell our clothes or furniture; he is telling us to sell our soul over to one choice.

I was extremely fortunate that this choice was made easy for me, for while I was handling much money, I never was able to really have it. I kept trying to lay hold on it but it was very elusive. In life everything that I had attempted to lay hold on was elusive—my false image, everything. I was more fortunate here than the rich, young ruler for he actually had his riches. Riches in the hand must be harder to release than riches that are only in one's hopes.

Again, I was fortunate that a clear direction was made easy. The hope for the resurrection being real was a better bet for me than the other things that I had been trusting. It has been easy for me to let go of that which I clearly say to be folly. I just needed something new to hope for. With this new hope I could then move forward just as I had done in early years. The Bible, I think, calls this childlike faith. This childlike faith for me has gained much substance as it grows. I do not have to continually weigh its value and reality, because this faith has a substance that is too big to hold in my hands or to weigh. This faith has moved away from being something that is not visible to being that which now appears. Real mature faith proves the Scripture in Hebrews 11:3, which states that things that are seen were not made of things that appear. This faith comes from God through the word of God. It starts as a small seed, then becomes a blade, and then it turns into the full corn in the ear (Mark 4:28).

36

Purpose

The preceding chapter illustrates the significant role that hope plays in our lives. This chapter ties to this hope the all-important accompanying issue of purpose. Just as the Bible states in the book of James that faith without works is dead, so is hope without corresponding purpose. This matter is of such importance that our very fulfillment, happiness, and alignment in the perfect will of God are dependent upon our being successful in this.

Let's go back to the area of our hope. Let's look closely to identify exactly what our own hope is. We need to be specific here, and we need to be real. I can see only three possibilities in which hopes may be placed:

- hopes that are based right here in this world only

- hopes that are divided between this world and a heavenly life after this world

- hopes that are securely placed in a life in heaven after life in this world

As was stated in the first paragraph, this is big stuff that should be treated as such. In the event that you may be having difficulty identifying which of the three possibilities apply to your hopes, this may help. Look at what you do and where your mind dwells, and this will tell you where your hopes reside.

If your hopes are securely placed right here in this world, then your corresponding actions and thoughts will be here also. Those whose hopes are divided between here and heaven will have divided actions and thoughts. For those whose thoughts and hopes are in heaven, their corresponding actions will be directed toward the advancement of God's kingdom here on Earth. Life here on Earth will seem abnormal for those people who actually are aliens here on Earth.

Choices for those people in the first group are simple: Get all you can and can all you get. This is all there is so get it while you can. I've belonged to this group but have never belonged to the divided group. I guess the biggest problem for me was and is: How do I function in this present world when my thoughts are in another? This has not been easy.

Life for those whose thoughts and hopes are fixed in heaven face an extremely difficult reality: How can I serve the physical needs of myself and my family while being totally one with my life's purpose? Those who are fortunate enough to be allowed to operate in full-time ministry find this easier. Others who have the very same love for God and motives for advancing God's kingdom here on Earth may find themselves making tents for a living here. Tent-making is not usually a well-paying profession, and it is sometimes difficult to appreciate its value. When one's thoughts are in another world, the meaningful purpose of tent-making cannot be easily maintained. This is a very challenging situation.

It has been brought to my attention often that tent-making with the right attitude does pay better and is more pleasing than tent-making with a bad attitude. Whether our tent-making is in the right attitude or place or the wrong attitude or place, it will really only be tent-making. Before my coming over into the third group, I found that while being in the first group, the get-all-you-can group, I actually could be one with my work. It was who I was. In tent-making this will never be totally possible.

Here's a simple formula, which may express the hope/purpose issue:

Hope + Meaningful Purpose = Success and Happiness
Hope—Meaningful Purpose = Frustration and Unhappiness

Let's readdress the position of those people whose lives and hopes are caught between this current world and its trappings and that other world out there in the future. This position actually is not a chosen one; it is a settling for one. These people are the ones depicted in the seed parable who for this period of time in their lives are having trouble with the thorns and briars.

My former pastor in Albertville, Mike Johnson, helped my understanding greatly one Sunday morning. Mike opened up a totally new area of thought for me. The teaching was that there was a time which might be called the *beginning of repentance,* which is not always the time of our being saved. Being saved is the time when we have decided fully and have left no room to return.

There is a picture of this very process in the Old Testament. Moses, prior to the Israelites being allowed to leave Egypt, commanded each head of household to take an unblemished lamb and further inspect that lamb for imperfections. Once the lamb was selected it was then slain, and its blood was placed upon the doorpost of each house. This practice is called Passover. The significance of this teaching on Passover today is that we are to take this lamb, Jesus Christ, into our homes and lives for an inspection to see if this lamb is really right for us. We, at this time only, should be ready for baptism.

If my understanding of this principle is correct, we can now look back to the issue of the three possible places for our hopes in order to receive some clarity. I believe that there are ultimately only two valid types of hope: hope for this world and hope for the heavenly world. It might just take some time for some people to come to their point of destination.

What lessons can be learned from the connection between hope and purpose? As I proceed into the lessons, you probably already have surmised that any lesson that I have learned came late for me and after much frustration.

The biggest and most disguised deterrent to walking in God's purpose or will is our *ignorance.* Our hearts may be right, but blindness to certain truths will literally eat away our faith. Some truths that were hidden from me were:

1. God's will operates along the lines of our own hearts' desires and abilities.

2. God rarely calls us to move out into areas or callings that are not supported by our spouse.

3. Whether we are in full-time ministry or tent-making, we must be active players on the team. We must find the area where we are willing to do this.

4. The attitude of "I'm too good for this" will get us into a big hole.

5. The attitude that there are people holding us back does not hold water. We are the ones holding ourselves back. God is big enough to move people or things when the time is right.

6. Promotion of ourselves by making our own changes will lead us nowhere. The biggest deception that the enemy uses is that God has something better for us over there.

7. The big test for us is: Do we work with honesty and integrity? We will never be allowed to do things the world's way. We can't lie, cheat, or take advantage of the poor.

There may never be anything that I could share with you that would be of more importance than those above statements. These things were not learned when I first came to Jesus; they were learned the hard way over much time. If I could just give one other bit of advice, just relax and do not struggle. God is out there and He knows about it all. It will work out well for those who are called.

37

The Will of God

This chapter could contain keys to understanding the very reason for and the answer to the many years of frustration and even failure in my life. My hope is that I can connect here and be able to express some simple but deep things—things that can seem so simple that everyone should know them anyway, but for me I knew them from a distance until very recently. This subject gets to the very heart of the biggest area of all for those who truly seek the will of God. Actually, there are two wills of God, and I will explain them now.

In 1 Thessalonians 4:3 we read, "For this is the will of God, even your sanctification." That should be clear enough that this is the ultimate will of God. I've come down pretty hard in this book on the doctrine of "once saved, always saved." Let me give some slack on this now. If a person wishes to teach this doctrine, or if God has enabled him to understand some deep things about it, go to it. This is totally fine to do but sanctification is the will of God. If we miss this sanctification we've missed the whole purpose of God. That's enough on this. Can we all agree on this one thing? Sanctification is the will of God. If it serves a purpose for some people to know that God is no double-dealer, or no cut-and-runner, then let's do it. For me, I've known for a long time that it was I who was a double-dealer and a cut-and-runner, not God. Do you love me?

Now, moving on. The second will of God is that we operate personally within the bounds of His calling for our lives. God does have a best calling for each of us. Romans 12:2 states that we "be transformed by the renewing of [our] mind so that [we] may prove what the will of God is, that which is *good* and *acceptable* and *perfect*." This could be interpreted as these all being the same area of walking in God's will, but I don't see this in that way. Sanctification is the utter will of God. Walking daily in His approved area of our lives is this good, acceptable, and perfect will. This walk in His perfect will has been extremely difficult for me because of the fact that the sanctification of my life has been so difficult. I can see things now that were totally hidden from me even three or four years ago.

So, what can I say to make things better for those who may be following my old path? I've already stated the big thing—get sanctified. Do it as quickly as possible, and do not hold areas of impurity. With a clearer soul we can see things that allow us to walk in the acceptable or even perfect will of God. It looks as though I must have spent many years just doing the good will of God. The good will of God could even allow us to spend time down in Egypt.

What evidence can I give that all this is true? And if it is true, does it work? My father told a little joke that fits here very well. There was this agricultural expert visiting an old farmer one day. The expert began to ask some touchy questions of the farmer. The old farmer explained, "Listen here, fellow, I know how to farm a lot better than I'm farming." For me, just to tell those things means very little, but to show actual signs of God's power working through my life is something.

When I started this book I was holding the same wisdom and knowledge on these very matters that I have today. I had not acted upon this knowledge, however. I've spoken in this book about the area of one's personal anointing. I've finally internalized this information and have taken it now into my being and currently am acting upon it. When I started this book, I was settled down into making bricks without any straw way down in Egypt. In actuality, I was a furniture salesman working in a store that offered high-priced credit to poor people, mostly blacks. I could sell the furniture, which represents making a regular brick, but I hated the easy credit rip-off aspect there. I think that I've finally bottomed out. I got sick and tired of being sick and tired.

Here are a couple of factors that contributed to my trip down to Egypt. First, I truly believed for many, many years that I was supposed to preach. This was what I wanted to do down deep, and it was even given to me by a word of knowledge about eighteen years ago. I could go deeper into this but here's what is important. This word of knowledge may have been accurate and it probably was but it has not yet fully materialized. Today, I still enjoy preaching but not pastoring.

Our church offers a pretty sophisticated gifts analysis seminar, which Karen and I recently attended. Can you guess what I do not have either gifts for or the desire to do? I have neither of these to be a pastor. My score on these was at the bottom, along with the gift for leading singing. My actual gifts were in the areas of discernment, miracles, and faith. I still believe that the lady who gave the word of knowledge to me was speaking from God, but there is more to the picture than just preaching today. Today, in order to be called a preacher, one must also be a pastor; the two are not synonymous in all cases. Today, a pastor usually does not feel comfortable while speaking boldly to the people. I have no problem with this.

In actuality I was called to preach. I have been doing it everywhere I possibly can do it. The disconnect is that the things that I preach do not always fit well into today's system. It is the inconsistencies of that system when compared to the realities of those things which I know to be true of which I speak. Could God actually be with a man who exposes the errors of the system? I think you know the answer to this. There are two requirements for one to be able to do this: His heart must be right—not selfish, greedy, or unloving—and his words must agree with the Bible.

Now, back to the main issue—knowing the will of God for one's own life. Egypt is a hard taskmaster. One will begin to hear false messages while in the hot desert of Egypt. One such false message to me was that I was just like my father. I only would work hard at things that were fun and enjoyable. Hearing this false message, I then went too far in the opposite direction. I accepted this and struggled with it too long. It was a false message.

Here now is evidence of my coming finally to real truth. I am now once again in the fund-raising field with a very old buddy from Promar days, Bill Belcher. I've seen even now that I still have a spark for this and some gifts also. I've also begun writing, which is the same as preaching I suppose, but it's just on paper. I've also received a potential ministry as a volunteer for addiction recovery with my church. I'm now acting upon the knowledge that I acquired earlier. It has settled into my heart, not just my mind.

How could one stay in darkness for such a long time? It is because of the absence of truth. How can people follow some of the things that they follow? It is because of the same absence of truth. God has levels of wills. Our ability to know the vital truths and step out into them determine the will in which we may walk.

38

Mother Teresa

An issue emerged on the TV networks recently to which I feel compelled to respond. The issue was the exposure of the contents of some actual letters from the deceased Mother Teresa to some of her personal confidants. In the letters, Mother Teresa expressed her doubts about the very existence of God. A second newspaper article by a priest from her denomination shed more light onto the TV stories. In his article, the priest stated that this doubt from Mother Teresa persisted throughout her life, but in reality is shared by all clergy at various times.

Most people allow this type of attack on Jesus Christ and God to pass right by without notice. This same type of attack was successfully accomplished back in 1962 when the Supreme Court ruled against prayer in schools. The late senator Everett Dirkson once said, "A few billion here, a few billion there, and pretty soon you're talking about real money." The New Age intellectual supremacist movement has succeeded in causing doubt in the minds of Americans toward God. Prior to my coming personally to Jesus Christ, I just assumed that the wisdom of the Supreme Court was valid. God should not be proclaimed openly at public events. Upon hearing about Mother Teresa's doubts prior to my own experience with God, I thought that even the best servants of God did not really have personal contact with him, if there really was a God at all.

I can't speak concerning Mother Teresa's faith, but I do know of the motives and purpose of those behind the stories. Their purpose is to bring discredit to the work of Jesus Christ on Calvary and to belie His resurrection from the dead. When these two things occur, the Christian faith is gutted. It is exactly the same as all others, even the New Age religion.

The thing that the New Agers are not aware of is this: God *is,* and He has never been without His remnant. It really is not very important what those who will never be His might think. Two groups are important to me: those who have received Him and those who might yet receive Him. I care about these people.

It is senseless for me to delve again into all the reasons that I have never in twenty years doubted God's existence. I will admit that He is sometimes hard to understand, and He is also seemingly very distant at times. I have never entertained any thoughts that He does not exist. His mighty miracles and His presence through His Holy Spirit have settled this issue for me.

39

A Simple Solution

Recently, I watched a scientist on TV who is a Christian, not a Christian scientist. This man was explaining the creation of the earth. He explained this well, but there were other opinions on the very same subject that differed. How can we move from the various positions on absolutely everything under the sun to being unified and in love with our brothers? Today, people seem to be so dogmatic on issues that one feels a need to either accept a person's position wholly or reject it wholly. Is there a medium point between this extreme and the position of love and acceptance?

How can a doctrinal division between two positions be reconciled so that brothers may dwell together in harmony and unity? First Corinthians 11 explains how to do this. In verse 20, Paul explains that when the church comes together it is not the Lord's supper that is eaten. Verse 21 tells that each one takes his own food before his brothers get theirs. One is left hungry while the other brother is drunken. Later in verse 34, Paul tells that if any man is so hungry for God's truths that he must offend those other brothers who have not yet attained that very truth, then he should eat at home.

What Paul is saying applies as much today as it ever has. The small things that we may have received from God should not spoil the big things. The big thing, and the only big thing, is in verses 24 and 25. In these verses, Jesus says, "Take, eat: this is my body, which is broken for you: this do in remembrance of me. This cup is the New Testament in my blood: this do ye, as oft as ye drink [it], in remembrance of me."

This walk with Jesus starts with Jesus' blood and His flesh being shed for our sins. It really ends with this also. The people who get sidetracked on issues are missing the main event. It's His blood being shed for our sins.

I am a simple man. I have been able to make the more complicated things simple in order to function. Two revelations have empowered me: the revelation of the magnitude of my sin and the revelation of Jesus up on that cross for that sin. This might have seemed too simple for me in my early walk, but I also failed much in those days. Today, these two facts dictate issues in my life. I was an ugly sinner and Jesus Christ went to the death on the cross for those sins. This works for me and I'd recommend it for everyone. Don't be too complicated. Take care of the big things first, and don't worry about the rabbit pills.

40

Cynic or Prophet

Obviously, there are calls for purity and holiness within my writings that may cause some people to back off. Some people will say that there is no way that a person can live like this today. Other people may say that there must be some secret sins that are not revealed. Both of these positions are partly true. To the first issue, that of living in purity, I confess that I am tempted just as all people. I do know how to get forgiveness, however. To the second issue, secret sins, I plead guilty also. I do have two nagging thorns in my flesh. The first of those thorns has crippled my ability to minister as a pastor. My role as a husband doesn't meet the required standards—the standards that are set in Ephesians chapter 5.

Have I prayed about this? Does it go away? Yes and no. Have I sought counsel? Have I studied Scripture? Yes, but it does not go away. It seems that major blemishes and flaws that operated earlier in my life still dominate the reality here today.

The second area of deficiency is that of my career, which has had much more than its share of ups and downs. Since becoming a Christian the downs have dominated the scene and I've found no remedy.

Now that these issues are out on the table, can a man with these glaring deficiencies be used today in any way by God? This type of thing is in no way being depicted in religious teachings today.

It seems to me that God does not often use pretty, neat, little messengers to get out the message of change. John Wesley was oppressed by his wife who screamed demonic sounds as he preached in the pastures. George Whitfield suffered similar conditions at home. These men were probably not the ideal husbands also. Evidently David and Moses must not have been either. Is it possible that my teachings with these glaring thorns could be from God, or are they just cynical thoughts?

The following is one possible answer to this question. If God wanted to get a fresh new message out today, how would it come? Would it come from the established means, or would it possibly be from a new, outside, and frail person? To get the answer we might look to see how God did this in times past. Men like Elijah, Elisha, Isaiah, Jeremiah, Hosea, John the Baptist, and even Jesus were not of the establishment. The disciples Peter, John, James, and Paul were not of the establishment either. It seems that God likes to use a flawed vessel who is willing to speak against established norms in a clear, direct, and bold manner.

My life for twenty years as a Christian can be easily discredited when the standards of career and husband are applied. If I failed to be honest and truthful on these matters there would be no need to send this book out. I'm not going any deeper now into these matters; I'm just admitting that if one looks only at these areas he will not find real success. Those who choose to do this will have ample evidence to write off the entire message on this basis.

Could God look at things and actually do things differently than we might think? If I had been allowed to attend seminary as I had desired I may have ended up a denominational minister, although I would have run into trouble. Had I been allowed to be a school principal I may have settled for that and been more complacent. Had I been more successful in some of the sales jobs I may have gone back to seeking worldly things. Had Turning Point School been successful I certainly would have been different.

Speaking about Turning Point School, my small inner-city school for disadvantaged kids, there has never been anything that I desired to succeed in so much as this. The very next morning after the school had been forced to close its doors in shame, I went on my daily walk with my dog Carter. At this point in my life I had failed at Promar, failed in public education, failed at sales, and now failed at this. As I walked with Carter in the dark, I had a serious talk with God. On this occasion I made a commitment to God that went like this: *God, I've lost all credibility in this world, I can do nothing on my own, and there are very few who believe in me. God, I've come this far with you. I'm going to go on the finish.* That walk was approximately eight years ago, and I've stood fast to my word.

Are those messages that you see here in this book from God or from a cynical old man? You will judge this, but one thing that I have learned may help you: God does not do things as we would expect Him to do them very often.

41

Why Did It Take So Long?

In a preceding chapter, I discussed two thorns in the flesh that God allowed to remain in my life for over twenty years as I steadfastly tried to follow Him. This is neither bragging about my steadfast following of God nor is it making excuses for the thorns remaining. This is just what happened. It is just what it is. It is possible that God has allowed the thorns to remain to act as a constant means by which to perfect sanctification. This would be a good thing.

To answer the question at the top of this chapter—Why did it take so long?—it really only took this time for the sanctification to occur. I've belonged to God the entire time. I think that this example helps to clarify the issue of eternal security for the true believer. God gets us through.

Will these thorns ever be removed? I sure hope so, but it is possible that they won't. Have I grown in faith and obedience because of them? To answer this, let me say that I do not have adequate ability with words to address this properly. Nothing that I could think of could have ever brought me to my current level of sanctification except these two issues. These two issues attacked the very base of my old support system, false pride.

Again, not to appear to be puffed up with my current level of sanctification, but let me say that I am a recent convert to much of it. In my early years as a Christian, I did some stupid things all in the name of loving God. I can remember how I fought and struggled with anger at things that occurred in the school system. Also, I fought with anger as people within the mobile home industry stole my commission. I finally saw that it was my own attitude that was drawing all this. I was the one causing people to do bad things. This was God's way to get me on the right track with God's will for my life. God is bigger and deeper than most people think.

Here is the real point about this issue. When I came to God, I was a very messed-up guy. When I cam to Him, I was approved for salvation once I received God's Spirit at the Emmaus Walk at Camp Sumatanga, but I was still full of the old corruption inside also. Here was a new convert to the Lord with two natures, God's Spirit within my spirit and my old soulish nature. If at any time God would have called me home during this time I would have gone straight to heaven, but I would have brought much junk with me. Identifying and revealing this very issue is my calling for life. Christians, don't try to take the easy way, *do it the right way*. There's much temptation today to just not go overboard, just be moderate with the Lord. Believe me, this is not God saying this to us.

42

To Whom Shall We Go?

Jesus had just stated to the Jews that if any man doesn't eat of His flesh or drink of His blood, they have no life in themselves. At this saying, many of Jesus' disciples turned away. Then, Jesus said to the twelve remaining disciples, "Will ye also go away?" Simon Peter answered, "Lord, to whom shall we go? Thou hast the words of eternal life. And we believe and are sure that you are that Christ, the son of the living God."

To whom shall we go? To whom shall I go? These questions were long ago settled for me. That time was right in the midst of my greatest attack and my greatest trial. My beloved company had been rocked, and my home had been severely shaken likewise. My life had been cut open. Where would I go?

As I sat for three and a half days at the Emmaus Walk at Camp Sumatanga in Gallant, Alabama, I heard the words of Jesus saying in essence, *If you come you must eat my flesh and drink my blood.* As I analyzed my current life and its circumstances and meditated upon and received those words, my decision was easy.

I had lived in this world for forty-four years. I had tasted the table of this world with its so-called delicacies. My decision was really no decision at all; it was not an analytical transaction or a hand decision. This flood of God's love, which came down over me during the entire three-day period, had swept me along as if I were in an actual flood. There was no decision. I must go with this flood.

This occurred in November of 1987. Believe me when I say that there have been plenty of opportunities to go back since then. I have never considered going back. The only consideration has been: *God, if I'm not doing something right, please show me how to do it right.*

I'd be surprised if there's ever been anyone who is more hardheaded than me, anyone who is a slower learner, and anyone who has made more foolish mistakes. I can honestly say that I've never considered going back. There are two things that have kept me going: the love of God and those words. *Jesus, you alone have the words of eternal life.*

In my life I've seen much. I've been to a Super Bowl, I've stood beside Coach Bryant, I've flown charter into Chicago, and I've been picked up by a limo. I've taken thirty people, expenses paid, to Maui. I've seen a lot and done a lot. These words of Jesus are not words from man. I've read great writings from man. These words are not from man. These words are from God. These very words alone prove the authenticity of God. These words are not only wise words, but they contain power within themselves to change lives.

I've been allowed to witness great things from God's hands, but no event can in any way surpass the greatness of God's presence through His word. My buddy, Ron Minton, and I once went to the hospital to visit an accident victim. My wife's maintenance man's son was involved in a serious accident, and upon arriving to see the family we were told that the teenager would die within a few hours. We left the hospital, went back to the office, and got down to some serious praying. At about 5:00 PM, which was four hours after we were at the hospital, I went back to visit the boy. As I walked into the waiting room I was told that one hour after Ron and I had left, the boy made a miraculous turnaround. He will now live. Is this just coincidental, the timing being one hour after we left the hospital? No. God heard the prayers of two men who had childlike faith to believe that He could really heal that boy. This and many other occurrences stand to prove God's existence, but they are not my main sources of strength. My main sources are that flood and those words. There have been plenty of opportunities to turn back. I might have taken one except for the fact that the flood swept me away. I don't know exactly where the stream will carry me here on Earth, but it will end up as Peter said. Where shall we go? You alone have the words of eternal life.

43

It's with the Heart

According to Romans 10:10, it is "with the heart a man believes unto righteousness." This book may have introduced a new theology, although it may be a theology from only one person. The key doctrine of this theology is that the kind of believing that God accepts starts with the heart and ends with the heart. Actually, the true end of this is a pure heart.

Along the way we face many temptations to fall away into works, legalism, or man's tradition. For a time, I believe that all who ever start with Jesus will fall victim to one of these. The proof of our faith is that after a time we will reemerge to true heart faith. God has given me the gift of discernment of spirits, which allows me to see into people's hearts. It is the humble, teachable, childlike heart that rings the bell. Let me say that the bell is not rung very often in a positive manner, but when it does go off you see a beautiful person.

Recently, my pastor taught a powerful lesson on Joseph and his long time of slavery. He made the point that in the real world, between the lines, Joseph probably was unable to appreciate his many setbacks to the point of living constantly in joy. In fact, I don't think that even God expects us to love being sent back to the dungeon for doing the right thing concerning Potiphar's wife. What God does expect is that over time our hearts are molded so that we not only see God correctly, but we see the relationships down here properly. When we come to this level we can rule with Jesus down here on Earth because we have now come to understand the process. This is a crucial point for us. If we never see the process we can never graduate to higher levels.

I think that if Joseph operated like many religious people today he would have been doomed. He would have spent his ammunition by proving his innocence and proving his righteousness. He could have gone all the way back to the eleven brothers who hated him because of his visions. Do you see? If he would have done this his visions never would have been accomplished. It is the attitude of heart that makes it through. Our knowledge, wisdom, talents, and sacrifices are all as filthy rags to God. The process is Attitude Development 101.

When our hearts have been fully developed over time and through all manner of testing, we will be able to show forth the fruit of the Spirit (Galatians 12:22–23). These attributes cannot be faked and are the mark of mature fruitfulness in God's kingdom. Look at these: love, joy, peace, long suffering, gentleness, goodness, faith, meekness, and temperance. How about just the first four: love, joy, peace and long suffering? Isn't that quite a list of objectives? Ordinary everyday religion will not produce these qualities.

Here's a bold statement: Until God has produced these qualities here on Earth He has not succeeded. He may do it in only a very few people, but until this level of heart faith has been attained God does not succeed. I heard a teacher of end-of-time events speaking on TV recently. He made the statement about the event that we call "the rapture," saying that the common beliefs about the depths of it are incorrect. He said that the popular opinion is that on the day of the rapture, the world will be in chaos as the Christians are raptured. He stated that people now believe that airplanes will fall from the sky in droves, and cars and trucks will go out of control without drivers. He said that we're wrong to believe this. There will be a few planes that may crash and a few cars or trucks, but not nearly as many as are thought. If he is correct, then there are fewer believers than is now thought.

All of us have hope that this opinion is incorrect and that many, many are caught up in the air. For this to occur, however, God has to quickly work on hearts down here on Earth now, for it sure looks like the end of times could be near.

On the night when I returned to my father's hospital room after making my confession to God, my father and I had a wonderful talk. At one point I said to him, "It seems to me that God is losing." My father's response was, "No, not everywhere." I'm so thankful for my father. I can say that my father probably spoiled me forever for false or dead religion. He was a bold advocate with a pure heart.

I can remember another occasion that at the time made me feel uncomfortable. He was in his last two weeks of life, but had a clear mind. He had formed a friendship with another cancer victim in the hospital. The other guy was being dismissed that day, and my father felt compelled to witness Jesus to him. The other guy professed to be a Mormon. I can remember how uncomfortable I was at my father's boldness to witness to another dying man and to possibly offend the man. I now appreciate this.

I can remember one last occurrence. On the last Saturday before my father's death the next week, I rolled him onto the outside terrace at UAB Hospital. As I sat out with him in the sunlight and peace, I saw a meek, humble man. I saw the thing that God calls "the ornament of a meek and quiet spirit, which in the sight of God is of great price" (1 Peter 3:4).

44

Conclusion

It's now time to begin concluding what has become a very stimulating and exciting project for me. This book may not have great mass appeal, but I pray that my family, children, and grandchildren will give it very close attention. The lifestyle that this book reveals is not for everyone, but I pray that it will be chosen by those closest to it.

To begin wrapping this work up, let's start at the top, the world. During my lifetime there have been many threatening groups of people: the Nazis, the Communists, and now the Muslim terrorists. In no way do I minimize the dangers imposed by these groups. One of them is active today. Our biggest danger today, however, is ourselves. We have a soulish form of AIDS that affects the heart. It's a form of hardening of the heart. The condition is a contagious one and has been caught through a repeated exposure to materialism, sexual immorality, hatred, and the lowering of boundaries.

The world in general has always shown manifestations of the symptoms that I mentioned, but America has been somewhat immune until about the past fifty years or so. The telltale evidence of the presence of the disease is the lack of goodness, the presence of greed, the selfishness, and the evil. The condition of the patient is steadily deteriorating. There appears to be no mass immunization available. Only a personal one-to-one cure is possible.

Admittedly, in this book I've come down hard upon organized religion and I'm not backing down now. The condition of man can never be cured by any other program than that which sent Jesus Christ to the cross to die for the condition of man. Today, we have programs, or this or that group, which in reality have only found a formula that attracts people. This work, the salvation of man, does not lend itself to franchising or mass merchandising. The cure for man is to be caught—one man to another, not one system to a person. Are we believers supposed to participate in this? You bet we are, but we must know that there are potentially dangerous distractions out there, and we must be careful.

Now that I have started at the top with the world and then moved down to the church, now I will probably offend even the individual person. The biggest, most offensive thing that can be said to man is this: Did you meet God's requirement for your salvation? The sons of Ishmael are now attacking us Christians and Jesus this day for that very reason. Similar things have occurred throughout history.

Here's how I offend people: I say to them, "Did you receive the Holy Spirit when you believed?" (Acts 19:2). I have no excuses. I cannot water this down. Since the time when I believed, I did receive the Holy Ghost as Jesus calls it (Acts 1:5). I know that I received this Holy Ghost because He lives in me in a way in which I can sense His presence within my own physical senses and in my own spirit. God is no respecter of persons. If He sent the Holy Ghost to live in me in this way He will do it for anyone. His approval of me was due to the fact that He knew from the very foundation of the world that little Jerry Glover would come to Him one day and submit his life to Him. When I did this He gave me His Holy Spirit.

Now that His Spirit lives in me I now am able, with twenty years of experience, to walk in only some of His ways. I walk in these ways, not because He changed me instantly, but because over time I allowed myself to receive His word. By receiving His word and by being in love with God, I've worked out my own salvation (Philippians 2:12). He'll do this for anyone who does what I did.

Can I speak any more clearly? There is no shortcut, no quick fix. If we really ever were initially saved, then we will all proceed along these very same paths. These are not Jerry Glover's paths. It took me twenty years just to be able to explain them. These are God's paths, and they lead all who participate in them to a place of oneness (John 17:21–23). When this oneness is achieved, we will be able to show this world that God sent Jesus.

Being totally honest at this time, I have very little to offer other mature Christians. My calling is in one area: to help pull some out of the fire (Jude 1:23). In my years as a believer, I've just about seen it all. I've seen deception of almost every type. I've seen good people, people whom I love who have been deceived. Can they be pulled back? Evidently, Jude thought that this was possible. I'm through pointing fingers now. I'll just say that this life with God through Jesus Christ is not the same life that is being portrayed in many places. It's not a cookie-cutter proposition, and it will cost us our old lives here on Earth. The fringe benefit program, however, for both now and forever are out of this world.

You are coming very close to the end now, and it will not disappoint. As I was sitting with Karen recently in the Bright Star Restaurant in Bessemer, Alabama, one of the best and oldest restaurants in the state, the final inspiration to conclude this book unwound right before my eyes due to the presence of a very powerful personality type and his family, whom I will soon discuss.

Now, will you allow me to do some foundational work? About twenty-three years ago I attended an exclusive dude ranch, for the purpose of shedding some baggage. This baggage included an alcohol addiction, smoking, depression, and a multitude of other sins. This ranch was where many famous people regularly attended.

Upon arriving at the ranch, we all gathered at 5:00 PM for a fake cocktail hour. I noticed a guy there who looked like someone I'd seen before. He had two or three groupie types hanging around him. I walked over to him, and as I heard his voice I asked, "Aren't you Jimmy Dean?" Quickly, our eyes made contact and a friendship began. He was Jimmy Dean, the ex-country-singing cowboy and most recently the Jimmy Dean Sausage man. I think that Jimmy sort of liked my approach to him, but we had something else in common that enabled us to hit it off pretty well. We had similar personalities. Our styles were both natural, like my father, Coach Bryant, Coach Stallings, Lee Roy Jordan, and all the people who are easy for me to communicate with. All are naturals. Let me say that these people are easy for me to communicate with, not the only ones whom I love. Over the ten days or so that we spent there together, we found another guy or two like us. One guy was an oilman from western Texas and the other one a Wisconsin cattle farmer.

On Jimmy Dean's last day there, we were joined at breakfast by a newcomer to our group, a movie director from Hollywood. This guy had been a casual pop-in, but was not part of our group. He was just there on that day. Upon discussing the ambiance and the luxurious treatment that all guests receive while at the Ranch, Jimmy made a comment that this treatment and our being catered to in extremes were just a little too much. The director quickly replied, "Oh! This is just laissez-faire." By "laissez faire" he meant that we deserve this. It's okay to just enjoy it.

Now, back for a moment to the issue of being a natural. Being natural is just the way that some people are. They don't have to work at it. Two of the most natural guys whom I've personally known are Jerry Duncan, our ex-tackle and ex-color analyst on the Alabama radio network, and Coach Gene Stallings.

Karen and I lived in Dallas years ago. While there, a neighbor who had played in the Rose Bowl with Bob Griese, Bob Mangene, and me went to some high school football games. One night as we came into the stadium, I spotted Coach Stallings and some other Dallas Cowboy coaches. Being a long way from Tuscaloosa and not having seen Coach for over ten years, I approached him and reintroduced myself. When I did this, one would have thought that I was someone important. That's how a natural is; he doesn't care about one's state in life.

Now, let's move back into the Bright Star Restaurant where Karen and I were seated very closely to a family that we discovered to be a well-dressed, sharp-looking lawyer, his teenaged son, and his wife. We were seated so closely that we could hear every word they spoke. In essence, my inspiration for this concluding chapter came as I considered this point for our personal need to be real. Then, the bell rang as I saw this lawyer. This guy had a very familiar air about him, one that I've seen often in fraternity houses, country clubs, ladies' teas, and other stuffed-shirt affairs. The air is that of faking it to be something big. I've seen big before and it didn't have a need to put on airs.

My thought as I listened to this guy was this: My son Chris, a young, natural-style lawyer, will destroy this guy in court. Before a jury it is very important to appear as real as possible. It's helpful in doing this if you don't have to fake it. This ability to be real definitely pays dividends here in our lives.

My other two sons are equally gifted and sharp in their own fields. Chad now has completed his MBA and is advancing in the pharmaceutical industry. Scott, my oldest son, is perhaps following in his dad's steps as being an entrepreneur or small-business person.

Here now is the big finale, the big crescendo. While I was the head manager at the University of Alabama, Coach Bryant had sort of a tradition. Prior to each of the biggest games—a Georgia Tech game after the whiskey bottle affair in 1962, the Tennessee game anytime, and probably even the Auburn game—Coach would bring me two boxes of cigars to put away in our trunks. When we had won the game, I would go into the dressing room, open the trunk, and give the boxes of cigars to Coach Bryant. He passed the cigars out to every player present as the sign that things were done *the right way.*

There was always jubilation in a victorious locker room, not the one when we gave Tennessee a tie in 1965. None were as sweet as those special cigar locker rooms. These celebrations, even those following national championship-winning performances, were the seal of *doing it the right way*—not the easy way.

With over forty years of living now behind me since those great cigar-smoking locker room scenes, I've received the message and have appropriated it to real-life issues. The message was: *Those who play properly win.* Playing properly was selling out completely to a cause, leaving no room for uncertainty or vacillation, holding back nothing.

I was unable to make this type of commitment at that time. I was not the best student manager that I could have been. I'm now aligned with the coach of all coaches, even bigger than Coach Bryant. I have another chance on this team. I am even a player this time, not a manager. I've learned the lesson now. I may not be the first over that marine corps obstacle-course wall, and I may look beat-up and nasty, but I'm getting over it.

I'm going out a winner. I'm a real player now. My reality has come by my looking at myself and being real about my flaws. In this game, God's game, that's what we can call *doing it the right way!*

If you have persevered until this point, I would assume that I may have connected at some point the vital need that we be real, that we be authentic. Can I ask one favor of you now? Will you allow yourself to take a step back, even out of your own body if possible? Will you take a look inside that person who is you? Will you look inside to see if that person is hiding or concealing anything that should be revealed? You deserve to be known and seen as the person you really are. I've let down my mask. Will you join me? Things sure feel good while being clean and honest.

The qualities that are intended by God to be manifested here on Earth are pure qualities, free from denial, deception, and delusion.

Jerry may be contacted at jerryeglover@bellsouth.net

Special Thanks To

1. My father, who is now with God in heaven. Dad, thanks. You did it.

2. My mother, who in February joined my father. Thanks for putting up with so much from all of those men.

3. G.B. Beasley, Ben Pillitary, Harold Walker, Excell, Mary Hester, and all the others who put themselves into our lives through love and support.

4. Milford Sprayberry, Jim Porter, T.R. Reid, Ron Minton, Jacky Beck, and all those who worked on the Emmaus Walk #50.

5. My wife Karen of thirty-three years, who has suffered alongside me through almost all that I have mentioned. She is about the toughest person I've ever known. I just wish I hadn't caused this toughness to be needed so much. She's also a wonderful mother.

6. My ex-wife Lynda, who went through very much also, and believe it or not is very close to Karen and me now. That's another miracle.

7. My three sons. You're the greatest!

978-0-595-46958-1
0-595-46958-2

www.ingramcontent.com/pod-product-compliance
Lightning Source LLC
Chambersburg PA
CBHW021143070326
40689CB00043B/1097